Fresh Ways with
Desserts

TIME-LIFE BOOKS

EUROPEAN EDITOR: Ellen Phillips
Design Director: Ed Skyner
Director of Editorial Resources: Samantha Hill
Chief Sub-Editor: Ilse Gray

HOW THINGS WORK
SYSTEM EARTH
LIBRARY OF CURIOUS AND UNUSUAL FACTS
BUILDING BLOCKS
A CHILD'S FIRST LIBRARY OF LEARNING
VOYAGE THROUGH THE UNIVERSE
THE THIRD REICH
MYSTERIES OF THE UNKNOWN
TIME-LIFE HISTORY OF THE WORLD
FITNESS, HEALTH & NUTRITION
HEALTHY HOME COOKING
UNDERSTANDING COMPUTERS
THE ENCHANTED WORLD
LIBRARY OF NATIONS
PLANET EARTH
THE GOOD COOK
THE WORLD'S WILD PLACES

New edition © 1995 Time-Life Books Inc. All rights reserved.
This edition published 1995 by Brockhampton Press, a member of Hodder Headline PLC.
First published 1986 by Time-Life Books Inc,

ISBN 1 86019 051 0
TIME-LIFE is a trademark of Time Warner Inc. U.S.A.

HEALTHY HOME COOKING

SERIES DIRECTOR: Dale M. Brown
Deputy Editor: Barbara Fleming
Series Administrator: Elise Ritter Gibson
Designer: Herbert H. Quarmby
Assistant Designer: Elissa E. Baldwin
Picture Editor: Sally Collins
Photographer: Renée Comet
Text Editor: Allan Fallow
Editorial Assistant: Rebecca C. Christoffersen

Editorial Staff for *Fresh Ways with Desserts*
Book Manager: Barbara Sause
Assistant Picture Editor: Scarlet Cheng
Researcher/Writers: Jean Getlein, Henry Grossi
Copy Co-ordinators: Elizabeth Graham, Ruth Baja Williams
Picture Co-ordinator: Linda Yates
Photographer's Assistant: Rina M. Ganassa
Kitchen Assistant: Chhomaly Sok

European Edition:
Designer: Mary Staples
Sub-Editor: Wendy Gibbons
Production Co-ordinator: Maureen Kelly
Production Assistant: Deborah Fulham

THE COOKS

LISA CHERKASKY has worked as a chef in Madison, Wisconsin, and in Washington, D.C. She is a graduate of the Culinary Institute of America.

ADAM DE VITO began his cooking apprenticeship when he was only 14. He has worked at Le Pavillon restaurant in Washington D.C., taught with cookery author Madeleine Kamman, and conducted classes at L'Académie de Cuisine.

JOHN T. SHAFFER is a graduate of The Culinary Institute of America at Hyde Park, New York. He has had a broad experience as a chef, including five years at the Four Seasons Hotel in Washington, D.C.

CONSULTANTS

CAROL CUTLER is the author of many cookery books. During the 12 years she lived in France, she studied at the Cordon Bleu and the École des Trois Gourmandes, as well as with private chefs. She is a member of the Cercle des Gourmettes and a charter member and past president of Les Dames d'Escoffier.

NORMA MACMILLAN has written several cookery books and edited many others. She has worked on various cookery publications, including *Grand Diplôme* and *Supercook*. She lives and works in London.

PAT ALBUREY is a home economist with a wide experience of preparing foods for photography, teaching cookery and creating recipes. She has been involved in a number of cookery books and was the studio consultant for the Time-Life series *The Good Cook*.

ROLAND MESNIER, Executive Pastry Chef at the White House, Washington, D.C., received his training in France, Germany and England. Mesnier has won two dozen gold, silver and bronze medals for his pastry and sugar work .

FRANETTE MCCULLOCH has studied cooking at the Cordon Bleu in London and at L'Academie de Cuisine. She runs her own catering business.

NUTRITION CONSULTANTS

JANET TENNEY has been involved in nutrition and consumer affairs since she received her master's degree in human nutrition from Columbia University. She is the manager for developing and implementing nutritional programmes for a major chain of supermarkets.

PATRICIA JUDD trained as a dietician and worked in hospital practice before returning to university to obtain her MSc and PhD degrees. Since then she has lectured in Nutrition and Dietetics at London University.

Nutritional analyses for *Fresh Ways with Desserts* were derived from Practicaire's Nutriplanner System and other current data.

This volume is one of a series of illustrated cookery books that emphasizes the preparation of healthy dishes for today's weight-conscious, nutrition-minded eaters.

Fresh Ways with Desserts

BY

THE EDITORS OF TIME-LIFE BOOKS

BROCKHAMPTON PRESS

Contents

Summer Fruit Salad

2 Chilly Delights 49

Apple Sorbet with Candied Almonds

Rum-Soused Plantains with Oranges and Kiwi Fruits

Frozen Lemon Meringue Torte

Cherry Puffs

4 Dessert Cakes and Assemblies 107

5 Desserts from the Microwave 127

3 Light and Creamy Favourites 85

Amaretto Custards with Plum Sauce

Dessert's Eternal Role

No one needs a dessert. A fruit tart, a blackberry sorbet, a cheesecake are not likely to appear on any nutritionist's list of essential foods. Indeed, it is easy to obtain all the proteins, carbohydrates, fats and other nutrients required for a healthy diet without ever eating a dessert more complex than a slice of ripe melon. Yet for most people there would be something missing in such a regimen, an unassuaged hunger for the sweet taste, the pleasing aroma, the pretty artifice of a dessert — and the deep, abiding satisfaction it provides.

No other category of food highlights the psychological and aesthetic dimensions of eating so clearly as desserts do. The fresh tang of a strawberry-lemon sauce with strawberry halves provides its own unique delight, as does the quintessential mildness of a soothing custard. There is a gamut of textures to choose from — crunchy, creamy, dense, airy — in tantalizing combination with an even broader range of flavours. And there is diversity of temperature too — what other food can be served warm, at room temperature, chilled or frozen?

Be it pastry or pudding, crisp or smooth, icy or hot, the heart of a dessert's appeal is its sweetness. Experiments with newborn babies suggest that humans have an innate predilection for the sweet. Just a few hours after birth, babies express only mild satisfaction at the taste of water, and a slightly acid solution prompts them to screw up their faces. A sugar solution, however, makes them smile — perhaps for the first time.

Desserts are the prime foods of festivity. What wedding or birthday would be complete without its cake, what Christmas without its pudding? Desserts, in short, make us feel good.

Controlling ingredients

The desires that desserts so abundantly fulfil can be accommodated without compromising the goal of healthy eating. The 120 desserts in this volume, which have been created and tested in the Time-Life Books kitchens, are intended to successfully round out a meal. With moderation and balance as a guide in menu planning, you can always find a place for dessert at the table — especially if you prepare the desserts as directed here and serve them in the portions recommended, which average 175 calories. Indeed, nutritionists acknowledge that refined sugar in modest quantities is not harmful to a normal person's health though its sweetness tempts us to increase intake.

The recipes in this book strive to limit sugar, honey and other sweeteners to no more than two tablespoons per serving. (In some instances, such as among the frozen desserts, more sugar is needed to guarantee the proper end result.) Of course, sugar is not the sole caloric ingredient in a dessert. Surprisingly, a teaspoon of sugar contains only 16 calories. Fats such as butter, with about 33 calories per teaspoonful, weigh in at double that amount.

The fats in desserts — usually in the form of butter, cream or egg yolks — have traditionally made pie crusts flaky, mousses smooth, custards rich. All are of animal origin, however, and all contain saturated fats, which trigger a rise in the level of blood cholesterol, so strongly implicated in heart disease. But as the following recipes demonstrate, fats can be curbed without marring a dessert's appeal. Thus butter, cream and egg yolks appear in many of the recipes, but in moderate amounts — enough, certainly, to lend flavour or texture or both. Butter is generally limited to half a tablespoon (7 g) per serving; sometimes it is paired with polyunsaturated margarine to achieve flakiness in pastry without increasing saturated fat. Cream is by and large restricted to a tablespoon per portion, and a single egg yolk is divided among four servings.

Grand effects can be staged at little cost in fat. A custard can delight with fewer egg yolks than usual when the number of egg whites is increased. A small amount of double cream, whipped to twice its original volume, adds a rich look and taste but only 45 calories to the pumpkin mousse with lemon cream on page 102. In many instances, low-fat, low-calorie ingredients such as yogurt and buttermilk yield desserts that are every bit as delectable as those made with richer ingredients.

A similar stratagem can reduce the sugar in recipes. Even for some cakes, biscuits, pastries and frozen desserts, where sugar plays a crucial role, quantities can be cut without compromising taste or texture. The results are still sweet, but never cloyingly so.

Throughout this book, the emphasis is on fresh, natural ingredients bursting with good flavour. There are no artificial sweeteners, no non-dairy creamers, no imitation egg yolks. Nor is carob substituted for chocolate; though carob has a somewhat similar appearance and lacks saturated fat, its taste is very different. Unsweetened cocoa powder, produced by extracting fat from chocolate liquor, is used wherever it will not diminish texture and flavour. Oatmeal and nuts, strewn over a dessert as a garnish, provide protein, vitamins, minerals such as iron and phosphorus, and fibre — the carbohydrate that is believed to protect against cardiovascular disease and colon cancer. Whole-grain flours come into play, along with the more familiar white flours.

Flavour, not nutritional content, provides the incentive for including sweeteners in a dish. No sugar or syrup contains a significant amount of any nutrient. Honey, in particular, enjoys an undeserved reputation as a good source of minerals and B vitamins. However, all honeys share an attribute that makes them a valued ingredient in cakes, biscuits and pastries: they are hygroscopic, meaning they absorb water. A dessert baked with honey loses moisture more slowly and stays fresh longer than one made with another sweetener. On humid days, the honey may actually absorb moisture from the air.

The white sugars — granulated, caster and icing — have a similar taste but differ in use because of their varying textures. Brown sugars possess an earthy flavour that complements such assertive ingredients as grapefruit, raspberries and figs. Combining the lusciousness of maple syrup with the tartness of apples in a mousse (page 91) creates an intriguing balance of opposites.

The magic of fruit

Most of the desserts in this volume derive their special identity from fruit. The first of the book's five sections is given over exclusively to recipes that feature fruit, but you will find fruit as well in the four other sections on frozen desserts, airy and creamy desserts, dessert cakes and assemblies, and microwave cookery.

Fruit has many qualities to recommend it as a dessert base. It is, to begin with, inherently sweet. Natural sugar accounts for 20 per cent of the weight of a banana, and more than 60 per cent of the weight of a fresh date. For most fruits, the figure falls in the range of 10 to 15 per cent. (One food chemist has speculated that the word "lemon" has come to mean something unexpectedly faulty because it is a mouth-puckering aberration in its class, with a sugar content of only 1 per cent.) Despite their sweetness, most fruits are low in calories: weight for weight, they contain only one fifth the calories of sugars and syrups. Using fruits is an ideal way

to create desserts that satisfy the calorie limit this book seeks to maintain for individual servings.

Besides sweetness at a modest calorie count, fruits boast other advantages. They are good sources of fibre and, as a group, offer a whole alphabet of vitamins. Potassium and phosphorus are among the minerals that fruits contain, and they are remarkably low in sodium and fat. All of this nutritional bounty is wrapped up in packages of gorgeous colours and sculptured shapes, from the pale green contours of the honeydew melon to the shiny quilted oval of the blackberry.

Many of the recipes in this book call for fresh fruits only. When a frozen substitute will work almost as well, the recipe will say so. Frozen raspberries, blackberries and cranberries all yield excellent purées and sauces. Frozen gooseberries can be of good quality, and frozen rhubarb is an excellent alternative to the fresh stalks.

There are many different varieties of fruits available in the shops. No matter what the season, there should be several types available at their peak of maturity: strawberries in the spring, raspberries, peaches and cherries in the summer, apples in the autumn, and oranges, lemons and grapefruit in the winter.

If you purchase fully ripe fruits, plan to use them within a day or two of their peak, for a decline in quality soon sets in. (This is especially true of berries and grapes.) Most ripe fruits — including tropical ones — should be stored in the refrigerator to retard the shift into overripeness.

When only partially ripened fruit is available, keep it at room temperature out of direct sunlight. To speed the ripening process, pack the fruit loosely in a brown paper bag, then set the bag in a cool, dry spot and fold it closed. Check the contents of the bag every day and transfer the fruits to the refrigerator as they ripen. Containers made of glass, plastic or stainless steel are best for storage — some metals can impart an unpleasant taste. Wash the fruit or wipe it clean with a damp cloth just before serving or preparing it.

Fruit's finest hours

The trick in selecting perfect fruit is to learn to recognize when it is mature, or at the peak of its developmental cycle. No fruit should be picked before it is mature; if it is, it will fail to undergo the complex chemical process of ripening, in which starches are converted into sugar, and colour, texture and flavour evolve. Most fruits will ripen properly if picked at maturity, which allows them to be shipped long distances to market without ill effect. A few, however — notably grapes, raspberries, blackberries, strawberries, blueberries and citrus fruit — must ripen on the mother plant. The best guide to maturity is colour: if a fruit is green in whole or in part, it will not, in most cases, taste good. Again, exceptions exist — green bananas, for example will ripen properly. Some fruits, of course — greengage plums, and certain

The Key to Better Eating

Healthy Home Cooking addresses the concerns of today's weight-conscious, health-minded cooks with recipes that take into account guidelines set by nutritionists. The secret to eating well, of course, has to do with maintaining a balance of foods in the diet. The recipes should therefore be used thoughtfully, in the context of a day's eating. To make the choice easier, this book offers an analysis of the nutrients in each recipe, as on the right. Unless otherwise indicated, the analysis is for a single serving of the dessert. The counts that are given for calories, protein, cholesterol, total fat, saturated fat and sodium are approximate.

Interpreting the chart

The chart below gives dietary guidelines for healthy men, women and children. Recommended figures vary from country to country, but the principles are the same everywhere. Here, the average daily amounts of calories and protein are from a report by the U.K. Department of Health and Social Security; the maximum advisable daily intake of fat is based on guidelines given by the National Advisory Committee on Nutrition Education (NACNE); those for cholesterol and sodium are based on upper limits suggested by the World Health Organization.

The volumes in the Healthy Home Cooking series do not purport to be diet books, nor do they focus on health foods. Rather, they express a commonsense approach to cooking that uses salt, sugar, cream, butter and oil in moderation while employing other ingredients that also provide flavour and satisfaction. Herbs, spices and aromatic vegetables, as well as fruits, peels, juices, spirits and vinegars, are all used towards this end.

In this volume, a conscious effort has been made to limit the desserts to 200 calories per serving — the average comes to about 175 — and to restrict, wherever possible, the amount of total fat and saturated fat in the recipes. Occasionally, in the interest of taste, texture or even the successful cooking or

---

Calories **175**
Protein **4g**
Cholesterol **8g**
Total fat **4g**
Saturated fat **1g**
Sodium **15mg**

---

freezing of a dessert, the amount of sugar or fat has been increased.

When a dessert recipe exceeds the 200-calorie limit, the cook should give special consideration to the overall nutritional content of the meal that is being planned. It is usually possible to compensate for the dessert's greater calorie count by selecting the meal's other components wisely. In several instances, spirits are listed as optional, but they are not included in the analysis accompanying each recipe. The same is true of optional garnishes. It is up to the cook to judge the effect of these ingredients on the nutritional balance of the meal.

The recipes make few unusual demands. Naturally they call for fresh ingredients, offering substitutes when these are unavailable. (Only the original ingredient is calculated in the analysis, however.) Most of the ingredients can be found in any well-stocked supermarket. Any that may seem unfamiliar are described in a glossary on pages 138 and 139. To help the cook master new techniques, how-to photographs appear wherever appropriate.

About cooking times

To help the cook plan ahead, Healthy Home Cooking takes time into account in its recipes. While recognizing that everyone cooks at a different speed, and that ovens may differ in their temperatures, the series provides approximate "working" and "total" times for every dessert. Working time denotes the minutes actively spent on preparation; total time includes unattended cooking time, as well as time devoted to freezing or chilling a dessert. Because the recipes emphasize fresh foods, they may take a bit longer to prepare than dishes that call for packaged products, but the payoff in flavour, and often in nutrition, should compensate for the little extra time involved.

Recommended Dietary Guidelines

		Average Daily Intake		Maximum Daily Intake			
		CALORIES	PROTEIN grams	CHOLESTEROL milligrams	TOTAL FAT grams	SATURATED FAT grams	SODIUM milligrams
Females	7-8	1900	47	300	80	32	2000*
	9-11	2050	51	300	77	35	2000
	12-17	2150	53	300	81	36	2000
	18-54	2150	54	300	81	36	2000
	54-74	1900	47	300	72	32	2000
Males	7-8	1980	49	300	80	33	2000
	9-11	2280	57	300	77	38	2000
	12-14	2640	66	300	99	44	2000
	15-17	2880	72	300	108	48	2000
	18-34	2900	72	300	109	48	2000
	35-64	2750	69	300	104	35	2000
	65-74	2400	60	300	91	40	2000

* (or 5g salt)

apples, pears and figs among them — are always green skinned.

In judging the fitness of fruit, keep the characteristics of each type in mind. Here are some guidelines for selecting fruits:

Apricots. Avoid small, hard specimens — they are probably immature and will never acquire good flavour. Choose those with a lush orange colour.

Berries. Choose firm, dry berries with no trace of mould. Blackberries should be shiny and truly black, strawberries an intense, shiny red, raspberries brightly hued. Blueberries and bilberries should be veiled with a whitish, natural coating of wax called the bloom; because the bloom fades about a week after harvest, it is a sure sign of freshness. Currants should be round, plump and juicy. Red and white currants should have gleaming, translucent skins; blackcurrants should be a rich, deep colour. For most berries, size matters little. If you refrigerate such soft-skinned berries as raspberries for a day or so, store them in a single layer to keep bruises or mould from developing.

Cherries. Large, firm cherries are superior in flavour and texture. Look for dark shiny skins on sweet cherries.

Citrus fruits. Colour and size are not clues to flavour and juiciness. Instead, select fruits that are heavy for their size — an indication of abundant juice. Grapefruits should have thin skin; a pointed stem end suggests thick skin. Navel oranges are easier to peel and segment, but Valencia oranges contain more juice.

Figs. These delicate fruits must be picked ripe, kept under constant refrigeration and used quickly. Reject any that smell sour.

Kiwis. This fuzzy, brown, egg-shaped fruit has bright green flesh, tiny black seeds and a tangy flavour. Buy plump, firm fruit and ripen it at room temperature until its flesh yields slightly to gentle pressure.

Mangoes. There are several varieties of this sweet, fragrant fruit; the colour varies from yellow or orange to red, pink, purple or two-toned. Ripen mangoes at room temperature and use them promptly.

Melons. Choose a melon that is heavy for its size. The stem end should be fragrant and yield slightly to gentle pressure. A ripe honeydew's skin is velvety rather than bald and slick.

Nectarines. Choose firm specimens with high colour and allow them to ripen at room temperature for a day or two.

Papayas. These tropical fruits have the shape of a pear and the flavour and texture of a melon. They may be either light green or pale yellow, but they ripen to a golden yellow.

Peaches. Choose fruits for their colour — creamy yellow or yellow with a red blush — and a distinctive peachy aroma.

Pears. Look for firm, clear-skinned varieties.

Pineapples. Select firm, unbruised fruit with no soft or moist spots. You can tell that a pineapple is ripe when a leaf pulled out from the centre comes away easily.

Plums. For cooking, choose a variety of plum that has a purple skin and yellow flesh. The larger, dessert plums, with red, yellow or green skins, are delicious raw but are so juicy that they partially disintegrate when cooked.

The special uses of egg white

Another ubiquitous ingredient in this book is egg white. Unlike the yolk, an egg white is free of fat and cholesterol, and it contains only 16 calories. Egg white is a culinary marvel to boot, accounting for the wonderful lightness of meringues, soufflés and angel food cakes. When egg white is beaten, its elastic protein inflates in a foamy mass up to eight times its original volume.

Use uncracked eggs that have been refrigerated in their carton. Before you break an egg, especially if you are using it raw, rinse its shell to rid it of bacteria. To separate an egg, some cooks crack it into a hand and let the white run between the fingers into a bowl.

Egg whites can be frozen. In fact, an angel food cake or a chiffon cake will have a better texture if it is made with thawed whites — provided the eggs were fresh when you froze them.

Beating egg whites is simple, but its success depends upon several factors. Allow the whites to come to room temperature; they will whip up faster than when chilled. Be sure that bowl, beaters and whites contain not a speck of fat or yolk, which inhibit the formation of foam. Do not use a plastic bowl; it is virtually impossible to rid plastic of all traces of fat.

A copper bowl, on the other hand, will produce excellent results: a chemical reaction between the whites and the metal makes it hard to overbeat them and ensures that the whites will rise high when cooked. However, the whites should not be left in it for more than 15 minutes, otherwise they will discolour.

If you use a metal other than copper, or a glass or ceramic bowl, beat the egg whites until they are slightly foamy, then add a pinch of cream of tartar per white to guard against overbeating. When the whites reach the desired volume, combine them with the other ingredients *(page 103)*. Do not set beaten egg whites aside for long, lest the foam begins to subside. Be sure to refrigerate desserts containing raw egg whites, and consume them within two days; bacteria can multiply rapidly in them.

The final flourish

Whatever dessert you prepare and whatever the occasion, presenting it attractively makes the eagerly awaited finale of a meal even sweeter. You may want to unmould a bombe on to a platter for all to admire before slicing it into serving portions. Glass dishes show off the radiant colours of fruits or sorbets, while small bowls or plates create the pleasant optical illusion that a diner's portion is larger than it is. In serving a well-chosen dessert in the style it deserves, you will have fulfilled its timeless role, bringing the meal to a happy and most satisfying conclusion.

1

Fruit's Artful Simplicity

The natural sweetness and succulence of fruits make them the perfect basis for desserts. It is not an easy task to improve upon something that is — when freshly plucked from tree, bush or vine — beautiful, delicious, refreshing and also healthy. Such attributes demand that the cook use the lightest of touches in preparing fruit desserts, lest the essential appeal of the principal ingredient be lessened and the effort turned into an exercise in lily gilding.

The recipes in this section fall into three groups, one of which includes presentations of raw fruits prepared in remarkably uncomplicated ways. For the simplest of these desserts, the fruit requires little more than slicing and arranging, with a syrup poured over the top. Some recipes call for a sauce, often made from another fruit for contrasting colour and flavour. Naturally, such dishes require the freshest and ripest of fruits, and the utmost care in preparation to preserve their flavour and colour. Some fruits, such as apples, bananas, peaches and pears, contain colourless compounds called phenols that cause the fruit to turn brown when it is peeled or cut. Many of the recipes call for combining the fruit with citrus juice or another acid liquid as soon as it is cut to prevent this unattractive, though harmless, discoloration. Chilling the fruit afterwards further guards against the effect.

Fruit should be cut in such a way that the pieces retain some of their contours, and thus their distinctive look. Avoid cutting fruit into tiny dice that can be identified only by the palate — knowing what you are eating by sight as well as by taste heightens the pleasure of the dessert.

A short step removed from the raw fruit desserts are those that require light poaching in a sweet liquid. Care must be taken to cook the fruit over gentle heat just long enough to soften it, so that the fruit maintains its shape and full flavour. Use a non-reactive pan of stainless steel, glazed earthenware or enamel to avoid discoloration or a metallic flavour. When cooled and allowed to steep in its poaching liquid, the fruit acquires magnified flavour.

The desserts are rounded out by fruit tarts, and by cobblers and crumbles in which the fruit is baked with a topping of dough or crumbs, some of oatmeal. These desserts may be baked in individual dishes or in a single large one; in either case, the ovenware should be attractive enough to bring to the table.

Orange Slices Macerated in Red Wine and Port

Serves 8.
Working time: about 20 minutes
Total time: about 2 hours and 20 minutes
(includes chilling)

Calories **145**
Protein **2g**
Cholesterol **0mg**
Total fat **1g**
Saturated fat **1g**
Sodium **2mg**

6	large oranges	6
¼ litre	Beaujolais or other fruity red wine	8 fl oz
4 tbsp	sugar	4 tbsp
1	cinnamon stick	1
⅛ tsp	ground cardamom or allspice	⅛ tsp
6 tbsp	ruby port	6 tbsp
2 tbsp	currants	2 tbsp
2 tbsp	toasted shredded coconut	2 tbsp

With a vegetable peeler, pare the rind from one of the oranges. Put the rind into a small saucepan with the wine, sugar, cinnamon stick, and cardamom or all-spice. Bring the mixture to the boil and cook it over medium-high heat until the liquid is reduced to about 15 cl (¼ pint) — approximately 5 minutes. Remove the pan from the heat; stir in the port and currants, and set the sauce aside.

Cut away the skins, removing all the white pith, and slice the oranges into 5 mm (¼ inch) thick rounds. Arrange the orange rounds on a serving dish and pour the wine sauce over them; remove and discard the cinnamon stick. Refrigerate the dish, covered, for 2 hours.

Just before serving the oranges, sprinkle the toasted coconut over all.

EDITOR'S NOTE: *To toast the shredded coconut, spread it on a baking sheet and cook it in a preheated 170°C (325°F or Mark 3) oven, stirring it every 5 minutes until it has browned — about 15 minutes in all.*

Poached Apricots in Caramel-Orange Sauce

Serves 8
Working time: about 45 minutes
Total time: about 2 hours and 45 minutes
(includes chilling)

Calories **135**		
Protein **1g**		
Cholesterol **11mg**	8	large ripe apricots,	8
Total fat **3g**		or 16 small ripe apricots	
Saturated fat **2g**	2.5 cm	length of vanilla pod	1 inch
Sodium **4mg**	¼ litre	dry white wine	8 fl oz
	200 g	sugar	7 oz
	10 cm	strip of orange rind, 2.5 cm (1 inch) wide	4 inch
		fresh mint leaves for garnish	

Caramel-orange sauce

100 g	sugar	3½ oz
1 tsp	fresh lemon juice	1 tsp
12.5 cl	fresh orange juice	4 fl oz
4 tbsp	double cream	4 tbsp

Blanch the apricots in boiling water for 10 seconds, then immediately transfer them to a bowl filled with iced water to arrest their cooking. Peel the apricots as soon as they are cool enough to handle. Cut open the groove in an apricot, then gently prise apart the flesh just enough to remove the stone; ease out the stone. Press the edges of the apricot closed. Repeat the process to stone the remaining apricots.

Slit the piece of vanilla pod lengthwise. In a heavy-bottomed non-reactive saucepan set over medium heat, combine the vanilla pod with ¼ litre (8 fl oz) of water, the wine, sugar and orange rind. Bring the mixture to the boil, then reduce the heat, and simmer the syrup for 5 minutes.

Reduce the heat so that the surface of the syrup barely trembles. Add the apricots and poach them, covered, until they are just tender — 3 to 4 minutes. With a slotted spoon, transfer the apricots to a plate; discard the poaching syrup. Cover the apricots and chill them for 2 hours.

While the apricots are chilling, prepare the sauce. In a small, heavy-bottomed saucepan, combine the sugar with the lemon juice and 3 tablespoons of water. Bring the mixture to the boil and simmer it until it turns a red-dish amber — 5 to 8 minutes. Immediately remove the pan from the heat. Standing well back to avoid being splattered, slowly and carefully pour in the orange juice, then the cream. Return the pan to the stove over low heat and simmer the sauce, stirring constantly, until it thickens slightly — about 5 minutes. Pour the sauce into a small bowl; cover the bowl and refrigerate it.

To serve, spoon the chilled sauce on to individual plates and place the poached apricots in the sauce. Garnish each apricot with a mint leaf.

Orange-Banana Flowers with Caramel Sauce

Serves 6
Working time: about 25 minutes
Total time: about 40 minutes

Calories **260**
Protein **2g**
Cholesterol **0mg**
Total fat **1g**
Saturated fat **0g**
Sodium **1mg**

200 g	sugar	7 oz
6	oranges	6
2	large ripe bananas	2
½	lemon	½

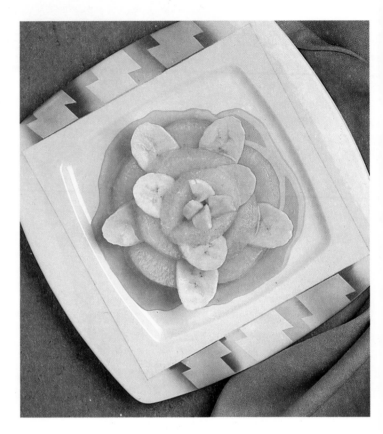

In a small, heavy saucepan, combine the sugar with 6 tablespoons of water. Bring the mixture to the boil and cook it until it turns a reddish amber. Immediately remove the pan from the heat. Standing well back to avoid being splattered, slowly and carefully pour in 4 tablespoons of water. Return the pan to the heat and simmer the sauce, stirring constantly, for 1 minute. Transfer the caramel sauce to the refrigerator to cool.

While the sauce is cooling, peel and segment the oranges as demonstrated below. Peel the bananas and slice them diagonally into pieces about 3 mm (⅛ inch) thick. Squeeze the lemon over the banana slices, then toss the slices to coat them with the lemon juice.

To assemble the dessert, arrange five orange segments in a circle on a plate. Place a banana slice over each of the five points where the segments meet. Arrange three orange segments in a loose circle inside the first circle, and place a banana slice over each of the three points where these segments meet. Top the assembly with two orange segments. Quarter a banana slice and arrange the quarters on top of the last two orange segments. Assemble five more orange-banana flowers in the same way.

Just before serving the flowers, pour a little caramel sauce around the outside of each one, letting some of the sauce fall on to the petals.

Segmenting a Citrus Fruit

1 *TRIMMING THE ENDS. To obtain segments free of pith and membrane from a citrus fruit (here, an orange), use a sharp, stainless steel knife and slice off both ends of the fruit.*

2 *CUTTING THE PEEL. With the fruit standing on a flat end, slice off the peel in vertical strips, following the contour of the fruit. Rotate the fruit after each cut, and continue to remove strips until peel and pith are completely removed.*

3 *REMOVING THE SEGMENTS. Working over a bowl to catch the juice, hold the orange in one hand and carefully slice between flesh and membranes to free each segment. Let the segments fall into the bowl as you detach them.*

Papayas and Melon in Sweet Chili Sauce

CHILI PEPPER ADDS SPARK TO THIS DESSERT.

Serves 8
Working time: about 30 minutes
Total time: about 1 hour and 30 minutes
(includes chilling)

Calories **155**
Protein **1g**
Cholesterol **0mg**
Total fat **0g**
Saturated fat **0g**
Sodium **8mg**

1	hot green chili pepper, halved lengthwise and seeded (caution, right)	1
12.5 cl	fresh lemon juice	4 fl oz
200 g	sugar	7 oz
2	papayas	2
1	cantaloupe or other melon	1

Combine the chili pepper, lemon juice, sugar and ¼ litre (8 fl oz) of water in a heavy-bottomed saucepan. Bring the mixture to the boil and cook it until it has reduced to about ¼ litre (8 fl oz) of syrup. Remove the chili pepper and set the syrup aside to cool.

Seed and skin the papayas and the melon. Cut the papaya into sticks about 4 cm (1½ inches) long and 5 mm (¼ inch) square. Cut the melon into 1 cm (½ inch) cubes. Mix the fruit with the cooled syrup and chill the mixture for at least 1 hour before serving.

Chili Peppers — a Cautionary Note

Both dried and fresh hot chili peppers should be handled with care. Their flesh and seeds contain volatile oils that can make skin tingle and cause eyes to burn. Rubber gloves offer protection — but the cook should still be careful not to touch the face, lips or eyes when working with chilies.

Soaking fresh chili peppers in cold, salted water for an hour will remove some of their fire. If canned chilies are substituted for fresh ones, they should be rinsed in cold water in order to eliminate as much of the brine used to preserve them as possible.

Fresh Fruit in Ginger Syrup

Serves 6
Working time: about 25 minutes
Total time: about 2 hours and 30 minutes (includes chilling)

Calories **150**
Protein **1g**
Cholesterol **0mg**
Total fat **0g**
Saturated fat **0g**
Sodium **3mg**

1	tart green apple, quartered, cored and cut into 1 cm (½ inch) pieces	1
2	ripe peaches or nectarines, halved, stoned and cut into 1 cm (½ inch) pieces	2
1	pear, peeled, cored and cut into 1 cm (½ inch) pieces	1
225 g	blueberries, picked over and stemmed	7½ oz
3 tbsp	fresh lemon juice	3 tbsp
2 tbsp	julienned orange rind	2 tbsp
5 cm	ginger root, cut into 5 mm (¼ inch) rounds	2 inch
135 g	sugar	4½ oz

Place the apple, peaches, pear and blueberries in a large bowl. Pour the lemon juice over the fruit and toss well, then refrigerate the bowl.

Pour 1 litre (1¾ pints) of water into a large, heavy-bottomed saucepan over medium-high heat. Add the orange rind, ginger and sugar, and bring the mixture to the boil. Reduce the heat to medium and simmer the liquid until it is reduced to about ½ litre (16 fl oz) of syrup. Remove the ginger with a slotted spoon and discard it.

Pour the syrup into a large bowl and let it stand at room temperature for about 10 minutes. Add the fruit to the syrup and stir gently to coat the fruit. Refrigerate the dessert, covered, until the fruit is thoroughly chilled —about 1½ hours.

EDITOR'S NOTE: *If blueberries are not available, bilberries, stoned cherries or seedless grapes may be used instead.*

Fig Flowers with Cassis Sauce

Serves 6
Working time: about 25 minutes
Total time: about 1 hour (includes chilling)

Calories **155**
Protein **1g**
Cholesterol **0mg**
Total fat **0g**
Saturated fat **0g**
Sodium **5mg**

½ litre	dry white wine	16 fl oz
1 tbsp	sugar	1 tbsp
4 tbsp	crème de cassis	4 tbsp
12	fresh figs	12
	fresh mint leaves for garnish	

Combine the wine and sugar in a saucepan over medium-high heat. Cook the liquid until it is reduced to approximately 17.5 cl (6 fl oz) — about 15 minutes. Pour the reduced wine into a bowl and refrigerate it until it is cool — approximately 20 minutes. Stir the crème de cassis into the cooled liquid, then return the sauce to the refrigerator.

With a small, sharp knife, cut a cross in the top of each fig, slicing no more than half way through. Carefully cut each quarter half way down into two or three small wedges, leaving the wedges attached at the bottom; each fig will have eight to 12 wedges in all. With your fingers, press the base of the fig to spread the wedges outwards like the petals of a flower in bloom. (More cutting may be needed to separate the wedges.)

Set two fig flowers on each of six chilled dessert plates. Dribble some of the sauce over the flowers, then garnish each serving with fresh mint leaves.

Peaches with Mint and Champagne

Serves 4
Working time: about 30 minutes
Total time: about 2 hours and 30 minutes

Calories **135**
Protein **1g**
Cholesterol **0mg**
Total fat **0g**
Saturated fat **0g**
Sodium **3mg**

6	ripe peaches	6
1	orange, juice only	1
1	lime, juice only	1
2 tbsp	honey	2 tbsp
4 tbsp	chopped fresh mint	4 tbsp
12.5 cl	chilled dry champagne or other sparkling white wine	4 fl oz
1	fresh mint sprig for garnish	1
	lime slices for garnish	

Blanch the peaches in boiling water for 10 seconds, then drain them and run cold water over them to arrest their cooking. Peel the peaches and halve them lengthwise, discarding the stones. Thinly slice eight of the peach halves lengthwise; transfer the slices to a bowl. Put the four remaining peach halves into a food processor or a blender along with the orange juice, lime juice and honey, and purée the mixture. Blend in the chopped mint, then pour the purée over the peach slices. Cover the bowl and chill it for 2 hours.

With a slotted spoon, transfer the peaches to a serving platter. Stir the champagne into the purée remaining in the bowl, and spoon the purée over the peaches. Garnish the peaches with the mint sprig and the lime slices just before serving them.

EDITOR'S NOTE: *There is no need to buy a large bottle of champagne for this recipe; small bottles are available.*

Grapefruit with Grand Marnier

Serves 6
Working time: about 30 minutes
Total time: about 1 hour and 30 minutes (includes chilling)

Calories **225**
Protein **2g**
Cholesterol **0mg**
Total fat **0g**
Saturated fat **0g**
Sodium **1mg**

2	limes	2
2	oranges	2
2	lemons	2
4	grapefruits	4
135 g	sugar	4½ oz
12.5 cl	Grand Marnier or other orange-flavoured liqueur	4 fl oz

Use a vegetable peeler to pare strips of rind from the limes, oranges, lemons and grapefruits. Cut the strips into julienne. Halve the limes, oranges and lemons, squeeze out the juice and strain it. Pour the juice into a saucepan. Add the julienned citrus rind, the sugar, the liqueur and 6 tablespoons of water to the pan; bring the liquid to the boil. Reduce the heat and simmer the mixture until it is syrupy — about 10 minutes.

Peel the grapefruits. Working over a bowl to catch the juice, segment them *(page 14)*. Transfer the segments and their juice to a heatproof bowl. Pour the hot syrup over the grapefruit segments and refrigerate the bowl for 1 hour before serving.

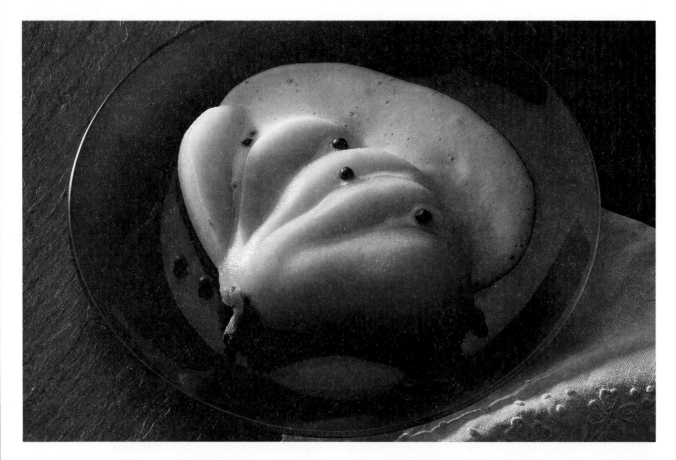

Peppercorn Pears in Sabayon Sauce

Serves 8
Working time: about 1 hour
Total time: about 2 hours (includes chilling)

Calories **180**
Protein **2g**
Cholesterol **70mg**
Total fat **2g**
Saturated fat **0g**
Sodium **19mg**

1	lemon, halved	1
4	firm but ripe pears	4
200 g	sugar	7 oz
¼ litre	dry white wine	8 fl oz
8	black peppercorns	8
2	eggs	2
½ tsp	pure vanilla extract	½ tsp
1 tbsp	brine-packed green peppercorns, drained	1 tbsp

Prepare acidulated water by squeezing the juice from one of the lemon halves into 1 litre (1¾ pints) of cold water. Peel, halve, and core the pears, dropping them into the acidulated water to prevent them from discolouring as you work.

In a large, shallow, non-reactive pan, combine the sugar, ¼ litre (8 fl oz) of water, the wine and the black peppercorns. Pare a strip of lemon rind from the reserved lemon half and add it to the pan. Squeeze the juice of the remaining lemon half into the pan as well. Bring the liquid to the boil, then reduce the heat to low, and simmer the mixture for 5 minutes.

Transfer the pears to the sugar syrup and poach them in a single layer for about 3 minutes on each side. With a slotted spoon, transfer the pears to a plate.

Continue to simmer the poaching liquid over low heat until it is reduced to about ¼ litre (8 fl oz) of heavy syrup — 5 to 10 minutes. Remove the peppercorns and rind with a spoon. Reserve 6 tablespoons of the syrup; pour the remainder over the pears, cover them and refrigerate them until they are chilled — about 1 hour.

Let the reserved syrup cool for 5 minutes, then use it to prepare the sabayon sauce. Whisk the eggs in a small, heavy-bottomed saucepan. Pour the syrup into the pan in a thin, steady stream, whisking constantly so that its heat does not curdle the eggs. Cook the mixture over medium heat, stirring constantly until it coats the back of the spoon — 3 to 4 minutes. Transfer the custard to a bowl. With an electric mixer set on high, whip the sauce until it has quadrupled in volume and is cool — about 5 minutes. Blend in the vanilla extract, then refrigerate the sabayon sauce, covered, until it is chilled — about 1 hour.

When the pears are chilled, cut them into fans: set a pear half core side down on the work surface. Holding the knife at a 45-degree angle to the work surface, cut the pear half into five lengthwise slices, leaving the slices attached at the stem end. Gently transfer the pear half to a dessert plate, then spread out the slices in the shape of a fan. Repeat the process to make eight fans in all. Spoon about 1 tablespoon of the chilled sabayon sauce next to each portion. Sprinkle each fan with a few green peppercorns and serve at once.

Plums with Cream

Serves 6
Working time: about 20 minutes
Total time: about 1 hour and 15 minutes
(includes chilling)

Calories **135**
Protein **1g**
Cholesterol **9mg**
Total fat **3g**
Saturated fat **2g**
Sodium **8mg**

750 g	ripe purple plums, halved and stoned	1½ lb
4 tbsp	sugar	4 tbsp
3 tbsp	arrowroot, mixed with ¼ litre (8 fl oz) water	3 tbsp
6 tbsp	single cream	6 tbsp

Combine the plums, sugar and the arrowroot mixture in a large, heavy-bottomed saucepan. Bring the plum mixture to a simmer over medium heat, stirring constantly. Reduce the heat to maintain a slow simmer and cover the pan. Cook the plums, stirring them from time to time, until they become very soft — about 20 minutes.

Transfer the plums to a food processor or a blender, and purée them. Strain the purée through a sieve into a large bowl. Ladle the purée into six small serving bowls. Cover the bowls and chill them for at least 30 minutes. Spoon 2 tablespoons of the cream over each portion and serve.

Strawberries with Lemon-Strawberry Sauce

Serves 8
Working (and total) time: about 45 minutes

Calories **155**
Protein **2g**
Cholesterol **70mg**
Total fat **2g**
Saturated fat **0g**
Sodium **19mg**

2	eggs	2
175 g	caster sugar	6 oz
4 tbsp	cornflour	4 tbsp
2	lemons, grated rind only	2
12.5 cl	fresh lemon juice	4 fl oz
1 kg	strawberries, hulled and halved	2 lb
1	carambola (star fruit), thinly sliced (optional)	1

In a heavy-bottomed saucepan, whisk together the eggs and the sugar; then mix in the cornflour, lemon rind, lemon juice and 12.5 cl (4 fl oz) of water. Set the lemon mixture over medium heat and stir it continuously until it comes to the boil. Continue cooking and stirring the mixture until it is quite thick — about 2 minutes more. Set the mixture aside to cool.

Purée 150 g (5 oz) of the strawberries in a food processor or blender. Mix the lemon mixture into the purée. To serve, spoon some of the lemon-strawberry sauce into eight dessert glasses or bowls. Carefully set the remaining strawberries in the sauce; garnish each serving, if you like, with carambola slices.

Summer Fruit Salad

Serves 6
Working time: about 25 minutes
Total time: about 1 hour and 25 minutes
(includes chilling)

Calories **190**
Protein **4g**
Cholesterol **2mg**
Total fat **2g**
Saturated fat **0g**
Sodium **35mg**

1	watermelon (about 3 kg/6 lb), cut in half crosswise	1
1	lime, juice only	1
1	orange, juice only	1
90 g	honey	3 oz
300 g	blueberries, picked over and stemmed, or other berries in season	10 oz
2	kiwi fruits, each peeled and cut into 8 pieces	2
¼ litre	plain low-fat yogurt	8 fl oz
2 tbsp	Grand Marnier or other orange-flavoured liqueur	2 tbsp

With a melon baller, scoop the watermelon flesh from the shell. Set the watermelon balls aside. (If you do not have a melon baller, remove the flesh with a curved grapefruit knife and cut it into uniform cubes, discarding the seeds.) Scrape out and discard any remaining flesh. Notch the rim of one shell half with a decorative zigzag and refrigerate the shell. Discard the other half.

To make the dressing, combine the lime juice, orange juice and half of the honey in a large bowl. Add to the dressing the watermelon balls, blueberries and kiwi fruits. Toss the fruit well, then refrigerate the salad for 1 hour.

To prepare the sauce, whisk together the yogurt, the remaining 2 tablespoons of honey and the liqueur. Refrigerate the sauce.

At serving time, set the watermelon shell on a large platter. Toss the salad once more to coat the fruit with the dressing, then spoon the fruit into the watermelon shell. Serve the chilled sauce in a separate bowl.

Apple-Prune Timbales with Lemon Syrup

Serves 6
Working time: about 40 minutes
Total time: about 1 hour and 10 minutes

Calories **140**
Protein **1g**
Cholesterol **5mg**
Total fat **2g**
Saturated fat **1g**
Sodium **2mg**

15 g	unsalted butter	½ oz
850 g	tart green apples, peeled, cored and cut into 1 cm (½ inch) pieces	1¾ lb
½ tsp	ground coriander	½ tsp
⅛ tsp	ground cloves	⅛ tsp
2 tbsp	fresh lemon juice	2 tbsp
4 tbsp	brandy	4 tbsp
125 g	stoned prunes, quartered	4 oz
60 g	sultanas	2 oz
4 tbsp	sugar	4 tbsp
1	lemon, rind only, finely julienned	1

Melt the butter in a large, heavy sauté pan over medium-high heat. Add the apple pieces, coriander and cloves, and cook the mixture, stirring constantly, for 5 minutes. Stir in the lemon juice, brandy, prunes, sultanas, 3 tablespoons of the sugar and 12.5 cl (4 fl oz) of water. Cook the compote, stirring frequently, until nearly all the liquid has evaporated — about 10 minutes.

While the apple compote is cooking, combine the rind, the remaining tablespoon of sugar and 4 tablespoons of water in a small saucepan. Bring the mixture to the boil, then reduce the heat to low; simmer the mixture until the liquid is thick and syrupy — about 7 minutes.

Spoon the apple compote into six 12.5 cl (4 fl oz) ramekins, tamping it down in order to give the timbales a uniform shape when they are unmoulded. Let the ramekins stand at room temperature until tepid — approximately 30 minutes.

Unmould the timbales on to individual plates. Garnish each with some of the lemon rind and dribble the lemon syrup over the top.

reduced by half — about 15 minutes. (There should be about 4 tablespoons of thick sauce.) Stir in the kirsch and the vanilla extract, then pour the sauce over the cherries. Grill the cherries for 2 to 3 minutes. Serve the cherries hot, with a spoonful of sauce dribbled over each portion.

Black Forest Cherries

Serves 4
Working (and total) time: about 30 minutes

Calories **225**
Protein **2g**
Cholesterol **20mg**
Total fat **7g**
Saturated fat **4g**
Sodium **75mg**

500 g	sweet cherries	1 lb
4 tbsp	sugar	4 tbsp
1 tbsp	unsweetened cocoa powder	1 tbsp
⅛ tsp	salt	⅛ tsp
4 tbsp	double cream	4 tbsp
4 tbsp	kirsch	4 tbsp
½ tsp	pure vanilla extract	½ tsp

Stone the cherries as shown on the right.

Combine 4 tablespoons of water with the sugar in a heavy saucepan set over medium-high heat, and bring the mixture to the boil. Add the cherries and stir gently to coat them with the syrup. Cook the cherries for 1 minute. Using a slotted spoon, transfer the poached cherries to a gratin dish or other fireproof serving dish, and set the dish aside. Remove the saucepan with the syrup from the heat.

Preheat the grill.

In a bowl, combine the cocoa and salt. Pouring in a steady stream, whisk the cream into the cocoa and salt. Stir the mixture into the syrup in the saucepan. Bring the sauce to the boil, then reduce the heat, and simmer the mixture, stirring occasionally, until it is

Stoning a Cherry

1 *INSERTING THE BLADE. Grip a swivel-bladed vegetable peeler on either side of the blade, avoiding the cutting edges. Insert the tip into the top of a cherry from which the stem has been removed, and work the peeler's curved tip round the stone.*

2 *REMOVING THE STONE. Wriggle the tip of the peeler back and forth to loosen the stone from the surrounding flesh. Then prise the stone up through the top of the fruit to dislodge it.*

Poached Peaches
with Berry Sauce

Serves 8
Working time: about 30 minutes
Total time: about 2 hours and 30 minutes
(includes chilling)

Calories **120**
Protein **1g**
Cholesterol **10mg**
Total fat **3g**
Saturated fat **2g**
Sodium **4mg**

8	firm but ripe peaches	8
½ litre	dry white wine	16 fl oz
200 g	sugar	7 oz
5 cm	strip of lemon rind	2 inch
8	mint sprigs (optional)	8
Berry sauce		
175 g	fresh or frozen blackberries or raspberries	6 oz
2 tbsp	caster sugar	2 tbsp
4 tbsp	double cream	4 tbsp

Blanch the peaches in boiling water until their skins loosen — 30 seconds to 1 minute. Remove the peaches and run cold water over them to arrest the cooking. When the peaches are cool enough to handle, peel them and cut them in half lengthwise, discarding the stones.

Put the wine, sugar and lemon rind into a large saucepan. Bring the liquid to the boil, then reduce the heat, and simmer the mixture for 5 minutes. Add the peach halves to the liquid and poach them until they are just tender — 3 to 5 minutes. Using a slotted spoon, transfer the peach halves to a plate. Discard the poaching syrup. Cover the plate and refrigerate it for at least 2 hours.

To make the berry sauce, purée 125 g (4 oz) of the berries with the caster sugar in a food processor or a blender, then strain the purée through a fine sieve into a jug or bowl. Stir the cream into the purée.

To serve, arrange two peach halves on each of eight dessert plates and pour a little of the berry sauce over each portion. Garnish each serving with a few of the remaining berries and, if you like, a sprig of mint.

Rum-Soused Plantains with Oranges and Kiwi Fruits

Serves 6
Working (and total) time: about 45 minutes

Calories **200**
Protein **1g**
Cholesterol **10mg**
Total fat **4g**
Saturated fat **2g**
Sodium **4mg**

2	oranges	2
4 tbsp	caster sugar	4 tbsp
30 g	unsalted butter	1 oz
2	large ripe plantains, peeled and sliced diagonally into 1 cm (½ inch) pieces	2
6 tbsp	dark rum	6 tbsp
2	ripe kiwi fruits	2
1 tbsp	icing sugar	1 tbsp

Squeeze the juice from one of the oranges. Strain the juice into a small bowl and whisk the caster sugar into it. Set the bowl aside. Peel the second orange; working over another bowl to catch the juice, segment the second orange as shown on page 14. Set the segments aside. Strain the juice in the second bowl into the sweetened juice.

Melt the butter in a large, heavy frying pan over medium-high heat. Add the plantain slices and cook them for 2 minutes. Turn the plantains over and cook them on the second side for 2 minutes.

Pour the orange juice over the plantains and continue cooking them until the liquid reaches a simmer. Cook the plantains at a simmer for 2 minutes. Pour all but 1 tablespoon of the rum over the plantains. Turn the plantains over and continue cooking them until they are soft — 2 to 4 minutes more.

Remove the pan from the heat; with a slotted spoon, transfer the plantain slices to a fireproof baking dish. Reserve the liquid in the pan. Arrange the plantain slices in the dish, inserting the orange segments among them.

Peel and chop one of the kiwi fruits, and press it through a sieve into the liquid in the pan. Stir the sieved fruit into the liquid, then pour the liquid over the plantain slices and orange segments. Peel, quarter, and slice the other kiwi fruit; set the slices aside.

Sprinkle the icing sugar over the contents of the baking dish, set the dish below a preheated grill just long enough to melt the sugar. Garnish the dish with the kiwi slices. Dribble the remaining tablespoon of rum over all and serve immediately.

Blackberry-Peach Crumble

Serves 8
Working time: about 30 minutes
Total time: about 1 hour and 15 minutes

Calories **175**
Protein **3g**
Cholesterol **30mg**
Total fat **3g**
Saturated fat **1g**
Sodium **200mg**

6	ripe peaches	6
1 tbsp	fresh lemon juice	1 tbsp
4 tbsp	sugar	4 tbsp
500 g	blackberries, picked over and stemmed, or other berries in season	1 lb
Crumble topping		
90 g	wholemeal flour	3 oz
1 tsp	baking powder	1 tsp
¼ tsp	salt	¼ tsp
15 g	cold unsalted butter	½ oz
125 g	caster sugar	4 oz
1	egg	1
½ tsp	ground cinnamon	½ tsp
1 tbsp	wheat germ	1 tbsp

Preheat the oven to 190°C (375°F or Mark 5).

Blanch the peaches in boiling water until their skins loosen — 30 seconds to 1 minute. Peel the peaches and halve them lengthwise, discarding the stones. Cut each peach half into five or six slices. Put the slices in a bowl, add the lemon juice and sugar, and gently toss them together. Set aside.

To prepare the crumble topping, put the flour, baking powder, salt, butter and 100 g (3½ oz) of the sugar into a food processor; mix the ingredients just long enough to produce a fine-meal texture. Alternatively, put the dry ingredients into a bowl and cut the butter in using a pastry blender or two knives. Add the egg and blend it in — 5 to 10 seconds. The topping should have the texture of large crumbs.

Arrange the peach slices in an even layer in a large, shallow baking dish. Scatter the blackberries over the peach slices, then sprinkle the topping over the blackberries. Stir together the cinnamon, wheat germ and the remaining sugar, and strew this mixture over the crumble topping. Bake the dish until the topping is brown and the juices bubble up around the edges — 45 to 55 minutes.

EDITOR'S NOTE: *For added fibre, leave the peach skins on.*

Tropical Fruit Compote with Rum

Serves 8
Working time: about 30 minutes
Total time: about 2 hours and 30 minutes
(includes chilling)

Calories **187**
Protein **1g**
Cholesterol **0mg**
Total fat **1g**
Saturated fat **0g**
Sodium **2mg**

100 g	sugar	3½ oz
2 tbsp	fresh lime juice	2 tbsp
1	strip of lime rind	1
1	pineapple, peeled, sliced into 8 rounds and cored (below)	1
2	mangoes, each cut into 8 wedges and peeled (opposite)	2
3	bananas, peeled, each cut diagonally into 8 pieces	3
6 tbsp	white rum	6 tbsp
1	fresh mint sprig (optional)	1

In a small saucepan, combine 17.5 cl (6 fl oz) of water with the sugar, lime juice and lime rind. Bring the liquid to the boil, then reduce the heat, and simmer the mixture for 5 minutes. Pour the syrup into a bowl; remove the lime rind and chill the syrup for about 2 hours.

To serve the compote, arrange the fruit on a serving plate. Stir the rum into the chilled syrup, then pour just enough of the liquid over the fruit to moisten it. If you like, garnish the fruit with a sprig of mint. Serve the remaining syrup in a sauceboat.

Peeling and Slicing a Pineapple

1 *REMOVING THE TOP. With a sharp, stainless steel knife (here, a medium-sized chef's knife), slice off the pineapple's bushy green top. Turn the fruit round and slice off 2.5 cm (1 inch) or so from the bottom.*

2 *REMOVING THE SKIN. Stand the pineapple on end and slice off a strip of skin, following the contour of the fruit. Cut deep enough to remove most of the dark eyes. Continue slicing until all the skin is removed.*

3 *CUTTING SLICES. Cut out any of the eyes that remain. Place the fruit on its side and, steadying it with one hand, divide the pineapple into as many slices as the recipe calls for.*

4 *CORING THE SLICES. With a small biscuit cutter, as shown here, or an apple corer, firmly stamp out and discard the tough, fibrous centre of each pineapple slice. If you do not have a small cutter or a corer, remove the centre with the tip of a paring knife.*

Preparing a Mango

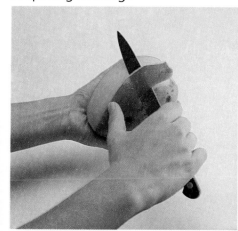

1 REMOVING THE PEEL. Cut a thin slice from the mango's stem end. Hold the fruit, stem side up, in the palm of one hand, and use a paring or a utility knife to peel the skin from the flesh, starting each cut from the exposed end.

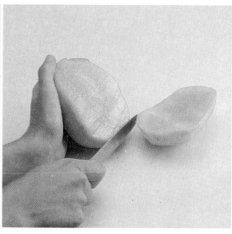

2 CUTTING AWAY THE HALVES. Stand the mango upright on its flat end and slice down one side — following the contour of the large, oval stone — to free one half of the fruit. Cut along the other side of the stone to remove the other half of the mango.

3 SLICING UP THE HALVES. Lay a half flat side down on the cutting board. Cut the fruit in half lengthwise, then slice each piece in half again to obtain the wedges called for in the recipe on page 28. (To obtain mango cubes, cut up the wedges and the flesh remaining on the stone.)

Strawberry Blossoms with Pears and Red Wine Sauce

Serves 8
Working (and total) time: about 45 minutes

Calories **225**
Protein **1g**
Cholesterol **4mg**
Total fat **3g**
Saturated fat **1g**
Sodium **5mg**

60 cl	red wine	1 pint
135 g	sugar	4½ oz
1.5 kg	firm, ripe pears, peeled, quartered and cored	3 lb
15 g	unsalted butter	½ oz
2 tbsp	fresh lemon juice	2 tbsp
750 g	strawberries, hulled	1½ lb

Combine the wine and half of the sugar in a heavy saucepan over medium heat. Cook the wine, stirring occasionally, until it is reduced to about ¼ litre (8 fl oz) — about 30 minutes. Transfer the sauce to a bowl and refrigerate it until it is cool.

While the wine is reducing, cut the pears into thin strips. Melt the butter in a large, shallow, heavy-bottomed pan over medium heat. Add the pears, lemon juice and the remaining sugar; cook the mixture, stirring frequently, until almost all the liquid has evaporated — 15 to 20 minutes. Transfer the pear mixture to a plate and refrigerate it until it is cool.

Set eight of the smaller berries aside. Stand the remaining strawberries on a cutting board and cut them into vertical slices about 3 mm (⅛ inch) thick.

Spoon about 4 tablespoons of the chilled pear mixture into the centre of a large dessert plate. Arrange some of the larger strawberry slices in a ring inside the pear mixture, overlapping the slices and propping them at a slight angle to resemble the petals of a flower. Form a smaller ring of strawberry slices inside the first and stand a whole berry in the centre. Repeat the process with the remaining pear mixture and strawberries to form eight portions in all.

Just before serving, pour a little of the red wine sauce round the outside of each blossom, letting a few drops fall on to the petals themselves.

Pineapple Gratin

Serves 6
Working time: about 20 minutes
Total time: about 30 minutes

Calories **170**			
Protein **2g**	1	large ripe pineapple	1
Cholesterol **45mg**	2 tbsp	raisins	2 tbsp
Total fat **1g**	2 tbsp	sultanas	2 tbsp
Saturated fat **0g**	5 tbsp	pure maple syrup	5 tbsp
Sodium **20mg**	3 tbsp	bourbon or white rum	3 tbsp
	1	egg yolk	1
	½ tsp	pure vanilla extract	½ tsp
	¼ tsp	ground ginger	¼ tsp
	1 tbsp	cornflour	1 tbsp
	2	egg whites, at room temperature	2
	2 tbsp	dark brown sugar	2 tbsp

Preheat the oven to 240°C (475°F or Mark 9).

Trim and peel the pineapple as demonstrated in steps 1 and 2 on page 28. Stand the pineapple upright and cut it in half from top to bottom. Remove the core from each half by cutting a shallow V-shaped groove down the centre, then cut each half crosswise into nine slices.

Overlap the pineapple slices in a large, shallow baking dish. Scatter the raisins and sultanas over the pineapple slices. Dribble 2 tablespoons of the maple syrup over the top, then sprinkle the dish with 2 tablespoons of the bourbon or rum. Cover the dish and set it aside at room temperature.

In a small bowl, blend the egg yolk with the vanilla extract, ginger, cornflour, the remaining maple syrup and the remaining bourbon or rum. In a separate bowl, beat the two egg whites until they form soft peaks. Stir half of the beaten egg whites into the yolk mixture to lighten it. Gently fold the yolk mixture into the remaining beaten egg whites.

Bake the dish containing the pineapple until the slices are heated through — about 3 minutes. Remove the dish from the oven and spread the egg mixture evenly over the fruit. Rub the sugar through a sieve over the top of the egg mixture. Return the dish to the oven and bake the pineapple until the sugar melts and the topping browns and puffs up slightly — about 5 minutes. Serve the gratin immediately.

Baked Plums with Streusel Topping

Serves 8
Working time: about 30 minutes
Total time: about 45 minutes

Calories **185**
Protein **2g**
Cholesterol **8mg**
Total fat **6g**
Saturated fat **2g**
Sodium **5mg**

8	ripe purple plums, quartered and stoned	8
¼ litre	brandy	8 fl oz
4 tbsp	dark brown sugar	4 tbsp
1	orange, grated rind only	1
	Streusel topping	
4 tbsp	oatmeal	4 tbsp
4 tbsp	plain flour	4 tbsp
30 g	unsalted butter, softened	1 oz
5 tbsp	dark brown sugar	5 tbsp
4 tbsp	finely chopped walnuts	4 tbsp
1	orange, grated rind only	1

Arrange the plum quarters skin side up in a 20 cm (8 inch) square baking dish. Preheat the oven to 200°C (400°F or Mark 6).

Combine the brandy, brown sugar and orange rind in a small saucepan. Bring the mixture to the boil, then cook it until the liquid is reduced to 4 tablespoons — about 5 minutes. Pour the brandy syrup evenly over the plums.

To make the streusel topping, chop the oatmeal in a food processor or a blender until it is as fine as flour. Transfer the chopped oatmeal to a large bowl and mix in the flour, butter, brown sugar, walnuts and rind. Dot the surface of the plums with spoonfuls of the topping. Bake the plums until the streusel has browned and the fruit juices are bubbling — 15 to 20 minutes.

Mixed Berry Cobbler

Serves 8

Working (and total) time: about 30 minutes

Calories **180**
Protein **2g**
Cholesterol **10mg**
Total fat **6g**
Saturated fat **3g**
Sodium **5mg**

250 g	fresh or frozen raspberries, thawed	8 oz
300 g	fresh or frozen blackberries, thawed	10 oz
300 g	fresh or frozen blueberries, thawed, or other berries	10 oz
4 tbsp	fresh lemon juice	4 tbsp
4 tbsp	sugar	4 tbsp
Oatmeal topping		
100 g	rolled oats	3½ oz
4 tbsp	dark brown sugar	4 tbsp
45 g	unsalted butter	1½ oz

Preheat the oven to 180°C (350°F or Mark 4).

To prepare the topping, combine the oats and brown sugar in a small bowl. Spread the mixture in a baking tin and bake it until it turns light brown — 8 to 10 minutes. Cut the butter into small pieces and scatter them in the tin. Return the tin to the oven until the butter has melted — about 1 minute. Stir the oats to coat them with the butter and bake the mixture for 5 minutes more. Set the oatmeal topping aside to cool. (The topping may be made ahead and stored, tightly covered, for several days.)

Put half of each of the berries into a large bowl and set them aside. Combine the lemon juice with the sugar in a saucepan and bring the mixture to the boil. Add the remaining blueberries to the syrup; reduce the heat to low and cook the fruit for 3 minutes. Add the remaining raspberries along with the remaining blackberries. Bring the mixture to a simmer and cook it, stirring constantly, for 3 minutes. Pour the cooked fruit into a sieve set over the bowl of reserved berries; use the back of a wooden spoon to press the fruit through the sieve. Stir gently to coat the whole berries with the sauce.

To serve, spoon the warm fruit mixture into individual ramekins or small bowls. Sprinkle some of the topping over each portion.

EDITOR'S NOTE: *If you prefer not to add the oatmeal topping, the fruit mixture may be served on its own, or it may be spooned over frozen yogurt.*

Ricotta-Stuffed Pears in Apricot Sauce

Serves 4
Working time: about 30 minutes
Total time: about 1 hour and 15 minutes

Calories **315**
Protein **5g**
Cholesterol **10mg**
Total fat **4g**
Saturated fat **1g**
Sodium **45mg**

½ litre	dry white wine	16 fl oz
125 g	sugar	4 oz
4	large firm but ripe pears	4
½	lemon	½
150 g	fresh apricots, or 60 g (2 oz) dried apricots	5 oz
125 g	low-fat ricotta cheese	4 oz
15 g	plain chocolate, finely chopped	½ oz
4	chocolate leaves (optional; box, opposite)	4

Combine the wine, 100 g (3½ oz) of the sugar and ½ litre (16 fl oz) of water in a large saucepan over medium heat. Bring the liquid to a simmer.

Meanwhile, peel the pears, leaving their stems attached; as you work, lightly rub the cut lemon half over the pears to keep them from discolouring. Using a melon baller or a small spoon, core the pears from the bottom. Squeeze the lemon half into the saucepan, then add the lemon shell to the liquid.

Carefully lower the pears into the simmering liquid. Poach the pears, turning them after 5 minutes, until they are somewhat translucent — about 10 minutes in all. While the pears are cooking, prepare the apricots. If you are using fresh apricots, blanch them in boiling water for 30 seconds to 1 minute to loosen their skins, then run cold water over the apricots to arrest their cooking. Peel and stone them. Whether you are using fresh or dried apricots, coarsely chop them.

Remove the pears from the poaching liquid with a slotted spoon and set them upright on a plate to drain. Refrigerate the pears. Reserve ½ litre (16 fl oz) of the liquid and discard the rest.

Add all but 2 tablespoons of the chopped apricots to the poaching liquid. Continue simmering the liquid until it is reduced to approximately 17.5 cl (6 fl oz) — about 15 minutes. Purée the apricots and the liquid in a food processor or a blender. Refrigerate the purée.

While the poaching liquid is reducing, mix together the ricotta, the chocolate and the remaining sugar. Finely chop the reserved 2 tablespoons of chopped apricots and stir them in. Put the ricotta mixture into the refrigerator to chill.

To serve, fill each pear with one quarter of the chilled ricotta mixture. Pour some of the apricot purée on to each of four plates; set a stuffed pear in the centre and garnish the stem end with a chocolate leaf if you wish.

Chocolate Leaves

Makes 8 leaves
Working time: about 20 minutes
Total time: about 1 hour

Per leaf:
Calories **18**
Protein **0g**
Cholesterol **0mg**
Total fat **1g**
Saturated fat **1g**
Sodium **0mg**

30 g	plain chocolate, chopped	1 oz

Carefully wash, rinse and dry eight rose leaves, and set them aside. Put the chocolate into a ramekin or a cup. Fill a saucepan 2.5 cm (1 inch) deep with water and set the ramekin or cup in it; bring the water to a simmer. As soon as the chocolate has melted, use a small, clean paint brush or other small brush to coat one side of a rose leaf with a generous amount of chocolate as demonstrated on the right. Set the painted leaf, chocolate side up, on a chilled tray or plate to cool. Coat the remaining leaves, then put the tray or plate into the freezer until the chocolate hardens — about 5 minutes.

Remove the chocolate leaves from the freezer. Working rapidly from the stem end, peel back a green leaf to separate it from the chocolate leaf. Return the chocolate leaf to the chilled tray. Repeat the process to separate the remaining leaves. Store the chocolate leaves in the refrigerator or freezer until shortly before use; they melt rapidly if the temperature of the room is warm.

EDITOR'S NOTE: *Leftover chocolate can be stored in an airtight container and reserved for another use.*

Making Chocolate Leaves

1 *APPLYING THE CHOCOLATE. Melt chocolate as directed in the recipe. With a small, clean brush, thickly paint one surface of a clean rose leaf. Set the leaf, chocolate side up, on a chilled tray. Coat all the leaves, then cool them in the freezer for at least 5 minutes.*

2 *PEELING THE LEAF. When the chocolate has hardened, remove the tray from the freezer. Working rapidly, gently pull the chocolate and rose leaves apart from stem to tip. Refrigerate the chocolate leaves until you are ready to use them.*

Nectarine Cobbler

Serves 8
Working time: about 30 minutes
Total time: about 1 hour and 20 minutes

Calories **285**
Protein **6g**
Cholesterol **40mg**
Total fat **4g**
Saturated fat **2g**
Sodium **175mg**

8	large ripe nectarines	8
6 tbsp	light brown sugar	6 tbsp
½ tsp	ground cinnamon	½ tsp
½ tsp	grated nutmeg	½ tsp
1 tbsp	fresh lemon juice	1 tbsp
2 tbsp	caster sugar	2 tbsp
Cake topping		
215 g	plain flour	7½ oz
1½ tsp	baking powder	1½ tsp
¼ tsp	salt	¼ tsp
100 g	caster sugar	3½ oz
15 g	cold unsalted butter	½ oz
1	egg	1
17.5 cl	semi-skimmed milk	6 fl oz
1 tsp	pure vanilla extract	1 tsp

Preheat the oven to 190°C (375° F or Mark 5). Halve the nectarines lengthwise, discarding the stones. Thinly slice the nectarine halves lengthwise. In a bowl, gently toss the slices with the brown sugar, cinnamon, nutmeg and lemon juice. Transfer the contents of the bowl to a large, shallow baking dish and spread out the nectarine slices in an even layer.

For the cake topping, sift the flour, baking powder, salt and caster sugar into a bowl. Cut in the butter with a pastry blender or two knives, blending the mixture just long enough to give it a fine-meal texture. In a separate bowl, mix together the egg, milk and vanilla extract, then pour this mixture into the bowl containing the flour. Using a fork, stir the mixture briskly just until it is well blended — about 30 seconds.

Dot the nectarine slices with evenly spaced spoonfuls of the topping, then smooth the topping so that it covers the fruit. Bake the cobbler for 20 minutes, then sprinkle the 2 tablespoons of sugar over the top. Continue baking the cobbler until the topping is brown, puffed and firm, and the juices bubble up around the edges — 20 to 30 minutes more.

Pears with Hazelnuts

Serves 4
Working time: about 30 minutes
Total time: about 45 minutes

Calories **225**
Protein **2g**
Cholesterol **8mg**
Total fat **8g**
Saturated fat **2g**
Sodium **5mg**

30 g	shelled hazelnuts	1 oz
4 tbsp	light brown sugar	4 tbsp
15 g	cold unsalted butter	½ oz
4	large ripe pears	4
½	lemon	½
1 tbsp	fresh lemon juice	1 tbsp

Preheat the oven to 190°C (375° F or Mark 5).

Spread the nuts in a single layer in a small cake tin or a roasting pan. Toast the nuts in the oven for 10 minutes. Test a nut for doneness by rubbing it in a clean tea towel; the skin should come off easily. (If it does not, toast the nuts for 2 minutes more and repeat the test.) When the nuts are done, wrap them in the towel and rub off their skins. Let the nuts cool to room temperature.

Put the nuts, brown sugar and butter into a food processor or a blender, and process them just until the nuts are coarsely chopped. Set the mixture aside.

Preheat the grill. Peel the pears, then halve them lengthwise, and core them, rubbing them with the lemon half as you work to prevent discoloration. Arrange the pear halves, cored sides up, in a large, shallow baking dish. Moisten the pears with the lemon juice and sprinkle the nut mixture over them. Grill the pears until the topping browns and bubbles — about 2 minutes.

Pear and Cranberry Crisp

Serves 8
Working time: about 30 minutes
Total time: about 1 hour and 10 minutes

Calories **190**
Protein **3g**
Cholesterol **8mg**
Total fat **5g**
Saturated fat **2g**
Sodium **2mg**

1	lemon	1
200 g	fresh or frozen cranberries	7 oz
6 tbsp	sugar	6 tbsp
4	pears	4
	Oat topping	
140 g	rolled oats	4½ oz
4 tbsp	unsweetened apple juice	4 tbsp
30 g	unsalted butter, melted	1 oz

With a vegetable peeler, pare the rind from the lemon. Chop the rind finely and set it aside. Squeeze the lemon, straining and reserving the juice.

Combine the cranberries with 4 tablespoons of the sugar, the lemon rind and 4 tablespoons of water in a saucepan over medium-high heat. Bring the mixture to the boil and cook it, stirring occasionally, until the berries burst — about 10 minutes. Set aside.

Peel and core the pears, then coarsely chop them. Transfer the pears to a heavy-bottomed saucepan. Dribble the lemon juice over the pears and bring the mixture to the boil. Reduce the heat to maintain a simmer, then cook the mixture, stirring occasionally, until the pears reach the consistency of thick apple sauce — 20 to 30 minutes. Set the pears aside.

Preheat the oven to 200°C (400°F or Mark 6).

For the topping, mix together the oats, apple juice and butter. Spread the oat mixture on a baking sheet and bake it, stirring occasionally, until it has browned — 20 to 30 minutes. Remove the topping from the oven and reduce the temperature to 180°C (350°F or Mark 4).

Spread about 2 tablespoons of the oat mixture in the bottom of a lightly oiled 1.5 litre (2½ pint) baking dish. Spread half of the pear mixture in the dish, then top it with half of the cranberry mixture in an even layer. Spread half of the remaining oat topping over the cranberry mixture. Repeat the layering process with the remaining pear, cranberry and oat mixtures to fill the dish. Sprinkle the remaining 2 tablespoons of sugar on top. Bake the crisp until the juices are bubbling hot in the centre — 20 to 30 minutes.

Apple Brown Betty with Cheddar Cheese

Serves 6
Working time: about 30 minutes
Total time: about 1 hour and 15 minutes

Calories **255**	6	firm wholemeal bread slices, crusts removed	6
Protein **5g**			
Cholesterol **11mg**	6	large tart green apples	6
Total fat **4g**	125 g	caster sugar	4 oz
Saturated fat **2g**	½ tsp	ground cinnamon	½ tsp
Sodium **170mg**	1 tbsp	fresh lemon juice	1 tbsp
	12.5 cl	unsweetened apple juice	4 fl oz
	60 g	mature Cheddar cheese, grated	2 oz

Preheat the oven to 150°C (300°F or Mark 2). Cut the bread slices into 1 cm (½ inch) cubes and spread them out on a baking sheet. Bake the bread cubes for 10 minutes, stirring them once to ensure that they cook evenly without browning. Remove the bread cubes from the oven and set them aside. Increase the oven temperature to 190°C (375°F or Mark 5).

Peel, quarter and core the apples, then cut the quarters into thin slices. In a bowl, gently toss the slices with 100 g (3½ oz) of the sugar, the cinnamon, lemon juice and apple juice. Spoon half of the apple mixture into a 1.5 litre (2½ pint) baking dish. Cover the apple mixture with half of the toasted bread cubes. Form another layer with the remaining apple mixture and then the bread cubes. Scatter the grated Cheddar cheese over the bread cubes and sprinkle the remaining sugar evenly over the top.

Bake the dish until the juices bubble up around the edges and the top browns — about 45 minutes.

Raspberry and Fig Brûlées

Serves 4
Working (and total) time: about 10 minutes

Calories **116**
Protein **1g**
Cholesterol **5mg**
Total fat **3g**
Saturated fat **2g**
Sodium **11mg**

125 g	fresh or frozen whole raspberries, thawed	4 oz
2	ripe figs, quartered, thinly sliced lengthwise	2
4 tbsp	soured cream	4 tbsp
4 tbsp	light brown sugar	4 tbsp

Preheat the grill. Divide the raspberries evenly among four 12.5 cl (4 fl oz) ramekins. Arrange one quarter of the fig slices in each ramekin, overlapping the slices as necessary to fit them in. Spread 1 tablespoon of the soured cream over the fig slices in each ramekin, then top each layer of soured cream with 1 tablespoon of the brown sugar rubbed through a sieve. Set the ramekins on a baking sheet and grill them until the brown sugar melts and the soured cream bubbles — 1 to 2 minutes. Serve immediately.

Baked Apples Filled with Grapes

Serves 8
Working time: about 50 minutes
Total time: about 1 hour and 40 minutes

Calories **165**			
Protein **1g**	8	tart apples, cored	8
Cholesterol **11mg**	¾ litre	Gewürztztraminer or Riesling	1¼ pints
Total fat **5g**	325 g	seedless grapes, picked over	11 oz
Saturated fat **3g**	½ tsp	ground mace	½ tsp
Sodium **5mg**	45 g	unsalted butter	1½ oz

Preheat the oven to 200°C (400°F or Mark 6).

With a paring knife, cut a ring of semicircles in the skin at the top of each apple; as the apples bake, the semicircles will "blossom" in a floral pattern. Stand the apples upright in a 5 cm (2 inch) deep baking dish and pour 12.5 cl (4 fl oz) of the wine over them. Put the apples into the oven and bake them for 30 minutes.

While the apples are baking, boil the remaining wine in a saucepan over medium-high heat until only about ¼ litre (8 fl oz) remains. Stir the grapes and mace into the wine, then reduce the heat, and simmer the mixture for 30 seconds. With a slotted spoon, remove the grapes from their cooking liquid and set them aside, reserve the liquid.

Spoon the grapes into the apples. Cut the butter into eight pieces and dot each apple with one piece of the butter. Pour the reduced wine over all and return the dish to the oven. Bake the apples until they are tender when pierced with the tip of a knife — 15 to 30 minutes more.

To serve, transfer the apples to individual plates. If necessary, use a knife to open up the "flower petals" you carved in the top of the apples.

Champagne Jelly
with Grapes

Serves 6
Working time: about 20 minutes
Total time: about 4 hours (includes chilling)

Calories **185**
Protein **3g**
Cholesterol **0mg**
Total fat **0g**
Saturated fat **0g**
Sodium **8mg**

750 g	seedless grapes, stemmed and washed	1 ½ lb
5 tsp	powdered gelatine	5 tsp
4 tbsp	sugar	4 tbsp
½ litre	chilled dry champagne	16 fl oz

Divide the grapes among six 17.5 cl (6 fl oz) moulds; the grapes should fill each mould no more than three-quarters full. (Alternatively, put all the grapes in a single 1.5 litre/2½ pint mould.) Refrigerate the moulds.

Pour ¼ litre (8 fl oz) of water into the top of a double boiler set over simmering water. Sprinkle in the gelatine and heat the mixture, stirring occasionally, until the gelatine dissolves. Add the sugar and stir until it too dissolves. Remove the gelatine mixture from the heat and pour it into a small bowl.

Set the small bowl in a larger bowl filled with ice. Stir the gelatine mixture until it has cooled to room temperature. Immediately add the champagne, pouring it against the inside of the bowl to preserve as many bubbles as possible. With a spoon, gently blend the champagne into the gelatine mixture. Ladle the champagne-gelatine mixture into the moulds; spoon the foam that rises to the top back into the bowl. Repeat the ladling and spooning process until the moulds are filled to their brims and all the grapes are covered by the liquid. Freeze the moulds for 30 minutes, then chill them for at least 3 hours.

At serving time, dip the bottom of a mould in hot water for 3 seconds; run a knife around the inside of the mould to break the suction, then invert a chilled plate on top, and turn both over together. Lift away the mould. (If the dessert does not unmould, hold the mould firmly on the plate and give them a brisk shake.) Repeat the process to unmould the other desserts and serve them immediately.

Strawberries and Melon in Fruit Jelly

Serves 6
Working time: about 30 minutes
Total time: about 2 hours (includes chilling)

Calories **115**
Protein **3g**
Cholesterol **0mg**
Total fat **1g**
Saturated fat **0g**
Sodium **12mg**

2½ tsp	powdered gelatine	2½ tsp
12.5 cl	fresh orange juice	4 fl oz
30 cl	fresh grapefruit juice	½ pint
4 tbsp	unsweetened white grape juice	4 tbsp
1 tbsp	fresh lime juice	1 tbsp
2 tbsp	caster sugar	2 tbsp
1	melon, halved and seeded	1
75 g	strawberries	2½ oz
1	kiwi fruit, peeled, thinly sliced crosswise	1
Strawberry sauce		
150 g	strawberries	5 oz
1 tbsp	caster sugar	1 tbsp
½ tbsp	fresh lime juice	½ tbsp

Put 3 tablespoons of water into a small bowl; sprinkle in the gelatine and let it stand until it has absorbed all the water and is transparent — about 5 minutes. Combine the orange juice, grapefruit juice, grape juice, the tablespoon of lime juice and the 2 tablespoons of sugar in a saucepan; bring the mixture to the boil, then immediately remove the pan from the heat. Add the gelatine mixture to the pan and stir until the gelatine is completely dissolved. Chill the fruit-jelly liquid just until it is syrupy — about 30 minutes —then keep it at room temperature.

With a melon baller, scoop out the melon flesh. Put three or four melon balls in a single layer into each of six 12.5 cl (4 fl oz) ramekins. Pour enough of the fruit-jelly mixture into each ramekin to barely cover the melon balls. Chill the ramekins until the jelly sets — about 20 minutes. Slice the 75 g (2½ oz) of strawberries in half lengthwise. Arrange some of the strawberry halves, their cut sides facing out and their stem ends up, round the edge of each ramekin. Fill the ramekins with melon balls, then pour in enough of the remaining mixture to cover the fruit. Chill the ramekins until this layer of jelly sets — at least 1 hour.

To make the strawberry sauce, purée the strawberries with the sugar and lime juice in a food processor or blender. Cover the sauce and chill it.

When the jelly is set, run the tip of a knife round the inside edge of each ramekin. Invert a chilled dessert plate over a ramekin, then turn them both over together and lift away the ramekin. Repeat the process to unmould the other desserts. Pour some of the strawberry sauce round each portion; garnish the desserts with the kiwi slices and the remaining melon balls.

Glazed Fruit Tartlets

Makes 16 tartlets
Working time: about 1 hour
Total time: about 1 hour and 30 minutes

Per tartlet:
Calories **120**
Protein **3g**
Cholesterol **5mg**
Total fat **4g**
Saturated fat **2g**
Sodium **110mg**

140 g	sifted plain flour	5 oz
30 g	cold unsalted butter	1 oz
15 g	polyunsaturated margarine	½ oz
½ tsp	salt	½ tsp
2 tbsp	caster sugar	2 tbsp
½ tsp	pure vanilla extract	½ tsp
2	ripe nectarines	2
300 g	redcurrant jelly or apricot jam	10 oz
125 g	fresh raspberries	4 oz
Cream filling		
175 g	low-fat cottage cheese	6 oz
1	lemon, grated rind only	1
2 tbsp	caster sugar	2 tbsp

Preheat the oven to 200°C (400°F or Mark 6).

To prepare the dough, put the flour, butter, margarine, salt and sugar into a food processor and blend just long enough to produce a fine-meal texture. Alternatively, put the ingredients in a bowl and use a pastry blender or two knives. Add the vanilla extract and 2 tablespoons of water, and continue blending until the mixture forms a ball. Shape the dough into a log about 20 cm (8 inches) long, then wrap it in plastic film, and chill it while you make the filling.

For the filling, purée the cottage cheese in the food processor or blender so that the curd is no longer visible, then blend in the lemon rind and the 2 tablespoons of sugar. Refrigerate the filling.

To form the tartlet shells, divide the dough into 16 equal pieces. Press each piece of dough into a fluted 10 by 5 cm (4 by 2 inch) boat-shaped tartlet tin or a fluted 6 cm (2½ inch) round tartlet tin *(opposite page)*. Freeze the tartlet shells for 10 minutes. Set the shells on a baking sheet and bake them until their edges start to brown — 6 to 8 minutes. Leave the tartlet shells in their tins to cool to room temperature.

Halve the nectarines lengthwise, discarding the stones, then thinly slice the nectarine halves. Melt the jelly or jam in a small saucepan over medium heat, stirring often to prevent sticking. If using jam, sieve it. Allow the mixture to cool slightly; it should be thick enough to coat the fruit.

To assemble the desserts, first remove the tartlet shells from the tins, then spread about 2 teaspoons of the chilled filling inside each shell. Arrange the nectarine slices and raspberries on top of the filling. Brush the fruit lightly with the warm jelly. If the jelly cools to room temperature, reheat it, stirring constantly, until it is thin enough to spread.

Lining Tartlet Moulds with Dough

1 *FILLING THE MOULD. After dividing the dough into 16 equal pieces, as called for in the recipe, press one of the pieces into a tartlet mould and spread it across the bottom with your fingers.*

2 *FORMING THE FLUTED EDGE. Gently force the dough up the fluted sides of the mould, using your fingers; with your thumb, press back down any dough that rises above the top edge of the rim.*

Gingery Peach and Almond Tartlets

Serves 10
Working time: about 45 minutes
Total time: about 1 hour and 30 minutes

Calories **150**
Protein **3g**
Cholesterol **60mg**
Total fat **6g**
Saturated fat **1g**
Sodium **35mg**

5	firm but ripe peaches	5
75 g	blanched almonds	2½ oz
4 tbsp	plain flour	4 tbsp
½ tsp	baking powder	½ tsp
½ tbsp	finely chopped fresh ginger root	½ tbsp
100 g	caster sugar	3½ oz
2	eggs	2
15 g	unsalted butter, softened	½ oz

Blanch the peaches in boiling water until their skins loosen — 30 seconds to 1 minute. Peel the peaches, then cut them in half, discarding the stones.

Preheat the oven to 170°C (325°F or Mark 3).

Put the almonds, flour, baking powder, ginger and sugar into a food processor or a blender; blend the mixture until the nuts are very finely chopped. Add the eggs and butter, and process them just long enough to blend them in.

Slice one of the peach halves lengthwise and arrange the slices in a lightly oiled 10 cm (4 inch) tartlet tin. Cut and arrange the remaining peach halves the same way. Spoon the almond mixture over the peaches and bake the tartlets until they are lightly browned — 30 to 40 minutes.

Let the tartlets cool on a wire rack, then remove them from the tins and serve.

EDITOR'S NOTE: *These tartlets may be made in a muffin tin.*

water with a wooden spoon or your hands. Encase th[e]
dough in plastic film and refrigerate it for 20 minutes.

Scatter several tablespoons of cornmeal over a clea[n]
work surface and roll out the dough to a thickness o[f]
about 3 mm (⅛ inch). Alternatively, place the dough be[t]
ween two sheets of greaseproof paper and roll it ou[t]
With a biscuit cutter, cut the dough into rounds abou[t]
11 cm (4½ inches) in diameter. Use the rounds to lin[e]
eight 7.5 cm (3 inch) tartlet moulds. Chill the moulds i[n]
the freezer for at least 10 minutes. While the moulds ar[e]
chilling, preheat the oven to 200°C (400°F or Mark 6).

Bake the tartlet shells until they have browned an[d]
are crisp — 20 to 25 minutes. Remove them from th[e]
moulds and cool them on a cake rack.

To prepare the tartlet filling, mix together the blue[-]
berries, sugar, lemon juice and lemon rind in a sauce[-]
pan. Bring the mixture to the boil over medium hea[t]
then continue cooking it until the berries have burs[t]
and there is about ¼ litre (8 fl oz) of juice in the pan –
5 to 7 minutes. Stir in the tapioca. Cook the filling, sti[r]
ring frequently, until it boils and thickens slightly –
about 10 minutes more. Set the filling aside to cool.

Spoon the cooled filling into the tartlet shells and le[t]
them stand for 10 minutes before serving.

Cornmeal Tartlets with Tapioca-Blueberry Filling

Serves 8
Working time: about 20 minutes
Total time: about 1 hour and 30 minutes

Calories **273**
Protein **3g**
Cholesterol **7mg**
Total fat **6g**
Saturated fat **2g**
Sodium **170mg**

175 g	plain flour	6 oz
60 g	cornmeal	2 oz
60 g	icing sugar	2 oz
½ tsp	salt	½ tsp
1 tbsp	cornflour	1 tbsp
30 g	cold unsalted butter, cut into 4 pieces	1 oz
30 g	cold polyunsaturated margarine, cut into 4 pieces	1 oz
Tapioca-blueberry filling		
600 g	fresh blueberries, picked over and stemmed, or frozen blueberries, thawed	1¼ lb
100 g	caster sugar	3½ oz
1 tbsp	fresh lemon juice	1 tbsp
2 tsp	grated lemon rind	2 tsp
1 tbsp	tapioca	1 tbsp

To prepare the tartlet dough, combine the flour, cornmeal, icing sugar, salt and cornflour in a food processor or a bowl. If you are using a food processor, add the
butter and margarine, and cut them into the dry
ingredients with several short bursts. With the motor
running, pour in 2 tablespoons of cold water in a thin,
steady stream, and blend the dough just until it forms
a ball. If the dough is too dry and crumbly, blend in up
to 1 tablespoon more of water. If you are making the
dough in a bowl, use two knives to cut the butter and
margarine into the dry ingredients, then incorporate the

Pears with a Spiced Walnut Crust

Serves 10
Working time: about 40 minutes
Total time: about 1 hour and 20 minutes

Calories **285**
Protein **3g**
Cholesterol **6mg**
Total fat **9g**
Saturated fat **2g**
Sodium **35mg**

60 g	shelled walnuts	2 [oz]
150 g	plain flour	5 [oz]
6 tbsp	light brown sugar	6 tb[sp]
30 g	unsalted butter	1 [oz]
30 g	polyunsaturated margarine	1 [oz]
¼ tsp	ground mace	¼ t[sp]
¼ tsp	ground ginger	¼ t[sp]
1	lemon, grated rind only	
½ tsp	pure vanilla extract	½ t[sp]
6	pears	
300 g	redcurrant jelly or apricot jam	10 [oz]

Preheat the oven to 190°C (375°F or Mark 5).

Spread the walnuts on a baking sheet and toa[st]
them in the oven until their skins begin to pull away –
about 10 minutes. Then allow the walnuts to cool [to]
room temperature.

Put the toasted walnuts, flour, brown sugar, butt[er]
margarine, mace, ginger and lemon rind into a foo[d]
processor. Process the mixture until it resembles coar[se]
meal. Sprinkle the vanilla and 1 tablespoon of wat[er]
over the mixture, and process it in short bursts just un[til]
it begins to hold together in dough pieces abo[ut]
2.5 cm (1 inch) in diameter. (Do not overprocess t[he]
dough lest it form a ball.)

Transfer the pieces of dough to a clean work su[r]
face. Rub the pieces between your fingers to fini[sh]

blending the dough, then put the pieces into a 23 cm (9 inch) tart tin with a removable bottom. Spread out the dough with your fingers, coating the bottom and sides of the tin with a very thin layer; crimp the top edge of the dough with your fingers. Put the tin into the refrigerator.

Peel, halve, and core the pears. Thinly slice each pear half crosswise, then arrange 10 of the pear halves around the edge of the tart shell, pointing their narrow ends towards the centre. Flatten each half, slightly spreading out the slices. Arrange the two remaining halves in the centre of the tart.

Bake the tart until the edges are browned and any juices rendered by the pears have evaporated — about 40 minutes. Set the tart aside to cool.

Cook the jelly or jam in a small saucepan over medium-low heat until it melts — about 4 minutes. If using jam, sieve it. Using a pastry brush, glaze the cooled pears with a thin coating of the melted jelly.

EDITOR'S NOTE: *If you do not have a food processor, grind the walnuts in a blender together with 1 tablespoon of sugar, then prepare the dough in a bowl with a pastry blender and a wooden spoon.*

2

Chilly Delights

Desserts that literally melt in the mouth are universal favourites, and go back to ancient times. Two thousand years ago, potentates everywhere from China to Rome refreshed their palates with frosty mixtures of fruit juice and snow or ice. Such chilly delights persist to this day, along with more elaborate versions containing fruit purée, egg whites, or fillips such as almonds, candied citrus peel and bubbling champagne.

Besides sorbets, which consist primarily of fruit juice, sugar and water, the following pages present recipes for frozen mousses, yogurts, parfaits, and even ice creams without the cream. The textures of these desserts range from the crunchily crystalline to the satiny smooth, but each one delivers sweetness and refreshment at meal's end with very little fat — and sometimes none at all.

Several freezing techniques are used. Sorbets are whisked by hand or blended in a food processor during freezing, so that their ice crystals remain small and air is drawn in. Both sorbets and ice cream may be prepared in a manually operated or electric ice cream maker; the more the mixture is agitated as it freezes, the finer the texture will be. This process, called churn-freezing, also draws air into the mixture and gives it a notable lightness. Because ingredients such as sugar and alcohol can hinder the freezing process if too much is used, do not exceed the amounts specified in the recipes.

Frozen desserts can generally be made a day ahead of serving. Beware, however, of storing them too long. No home-made sorbet, mousse or bombe will remain in prime condition for more than a few days at a temperature of −17°C (0°F) or lower; some, such as orange sorbet, have evanescent flavours and should be eaten on the day they are prepared. Before freezing highly acid fruit desserts, cover them with plastic film — their acid content can eat away at aluminium foil.

If a frozen dessert is too hard, refrigerate it for 20 to 30 minutes before serving time to let it soften slightly for easy slicing or scooping. Present the frozen dessert in well-chilled dishes to minimize melting — and, of course, to heighten the pleasure it offers.

Freezing Sorbets and Ice Creams

Frozen desserts count among everyone's favourites. Three different methods for preparing them are examined below. For efficiency, make sure that the dessert mixture is well chilled before you freeze it.

Hand-whisking method

This basic procedure involves placing the dessert mixture in a freezer, then whisking it from time to time as it firms up to break the ice crystals and aerate the mixture. Before starting, turn your freezer to its coldest setting. Use as large a non-reactive metal bowl as will fit into the freezer, or resort to metal ice-cube trays. (Vessels made of glass, a poor conductor of heat, will retard the freezing process.) Place the bowl containing the dessert in the freezer. When a ring of crystals about 1 cm (½ inch) wide has formed round the outside edge of the mixture, usually after 1 to 2 hours, whisk the mixture. Return the bowl to the freezer and allow another ring of crystals to form before whisking the mixture again. Repeat the whisking a few more times until the dessert is frozen through. After the final whisking, allow the dessert to freeze an additional 15 minutes, then serve it.

Food processor method

This fast and easy method utilizes a food processor once the dessert mixture has set. Freeze the mixture in a non-reactive metal bowl; when the dessert has solidified — the centre may still be soft — break it into chunks and place them in a food processor. (Return the empty bowl to the freezer; you will need it later.) Process the frozen chunks until the dessert has a smooth consistency; be careful not to over-process it or it will melt. Return the dessert to the chilled bowl and let it sit in the freezer — a process that cooks call "ripening" — for another 15 minutes until it firms up.

Frozen desserts consisting only of fruit juice and a moderate amount of sugar or those containing alcohol will melt faster than those made with fruit purée, a high amount of sugar, egg white, milk or yogurt. They should be broken into chunks, then processed quickly to break down the crystals without melting. Sorbets prepared according to the food processor method will keep, covered, for several days in the freezer; to restore their consistency, however, they will probably need reprocessing followed by 15 minutes in the freezer.

Churning method

The old-fashioned ice cream maker that demanded half an hour or more of laborious hand-cranking is quickly being replaced by electric and other convenience models, some containing coolants. In using them, be sure to follow the manufacturer's instructions carefully.

Blackberry Sorbet

Serves 6
Working time: about 10 minutes
Total time: 1 to 3 hours, depending on freezing method

Calories **225**
Protein **1g**
Cholesterol **0mg**
Total fat **0g**
Saturated fat **0g**
Sodium **7mg**

650 g	fresh blackberries, picked over or frozen blackberries, thawed	1¼ lb
250 g	caster sugar	8 oz
1 tbsp	fresh lemon juice	1 tbsp

Purée all but 90 g (3 oz) of the blackberries in a food processor or blender. Strain the purée through a fine sieve into a bowl. Discard any solids remaining in the sieve. Add the sugar and lemon juice to the purée, then stir the mixture until the sugar has dissolved.

Freeze the sorbet, using one of the methods described on the left. Just before serving, garnish the sorbet with the reserved blackberries.

EDITOR'S NOTE: *If you prefer the sorbet slightly tart, reduce the amount of sugar to 175 g (6 oz).*

Apple Sorbet
with Candied Almonds

Serves 8
Working time: about 50 minutes
Total time: 1 to 3 hours, depending on freezing method

Calories **250**			
Protein **1g**	10	tart green apples	10
Cholesterol **0mg**	5	lemons, juice only	5
Total fat **2g**	330 g	caster sugar	11 oz
Saturated fat **0g**	30 g	slivered almonds	1 oz
Sodium **2mg**	1 tbsp	brown sugar	1 tbsp

Cut off and discard the top quarter of one of the apples. Using a melon baller or spoon, scoop the flesh, core and seeds from the apple, leaving a 5 mm (¼ inch) thick wall. Reserve the flesh; discard the core and seeds. Sprinkle the inside of the apple and the reserved flesh with some of the lemon juice. Repeat the process with all but two of the remaining apples, then freeze the hollowed apples. Peel, seed and chop the two remaining apples, and add them to the reserved flesh.

Put ½ litre (16 fl oz) of water, 200 g (7 oz) of the sugar and about half of the remaining lemon juice in a saucepan. Bring the liquid to the boil, reduce the heat to medium, and simmer for 3 minutes. Add the reserved apple flesh and simmer it until it is tender — 3 to 4 minutes. With a slotted spoon, transfer the cooked apple flesh to a food processor or blender. Discard the poaching liquid. Purée the apple; put ½ litre (16 fl oz) of the purée into a bowl and allow it to cool. If any purée is left over, reserve it for another use.

Stir the remaining lemon juice and the remaining sugar into the apple purée. Freeze the mixture, using one of the methods on the opposite page.

While the sorbet is freezing, put the slivered almonds in a small, heavy frying pan over medium heat. Toast the almonds, stirring constantly, until they turn golden-brown — about 5 minutes. Stir in the brown sugar, increase the heat to high, and cook the almonds until they are coated with melted sugar — about 1 minute more. Set the almonds aside.

When the sorbet is firm, scoop or spoon it into the prepared apple cups, then sprinkle some of the candied almonds over each apple. Keep the apples in the freezer until they are served.

EDITOR'S NOTE: *These sorbets are best consumed within 24 hours of their preparation.*

Lemon Cups

Serves 8
Working time: about 30 minutes
Total time: 1 to 3 hours, depending on freezing method

Calories **50**
Protein **0g**
Cholesterol **0mg**
Total fat **0g**
Saturated fat **0g**
Sodium **0mg**

4	lemons, plus ½ tsp grated lemon rind	4
100 g	caster sugar	3½ oz
16	citrus leaves or fresh mint leaves (optional)	16

Halve the lemons lengthwise, cutting the rind in a zig-zag pattern *(page 56)*. Remove the pulp and seeds from the halves with a melon baller or a small, sturdy spoon. Transfer the pulp to a sieve set over a bowl, and press down on it with the bottom of a ladle or the back of a wooden spoon to extract all the juice. Discard the pulp and seeds and reserve the juice. Lightly pare the bottom of each lemon shell to stabilize it. Freeze the lemon halves.

Strain 12.5 cl (4 fl oz) of the lemon juice into a bowl. (Any excess juice may be reserved for another use.) Whisk 35 cl (12 fl oz) of water, the grated rind and the sugar into the strained lemon juice, stirring until the sugar has dissolved. Freeze the sorbet, using one of the methods described on page 50.

When the sorbet is firm, spoon or pipe it into the lemon halves and return them to the freezer. If you like, garnish each lemon cup with two of the citrus or mint leaves before serving.

Lime Cups

Serves 8
Working time: about 30 minutes
Total time: 1 to 3 hours, depending on freezing method

Calories **50**
Protein **0g**
Cholesterol **0mg**
Total fat **0g**
Saturated fat **0g**
Sodium **0mg**

8	limes, plus 1 tsp grated lime rind	8
2 tbsp	fresh lemon juice	2 tbsp
100 g	caster sugar	3½ oz
1	egg white (optional)	1
8	citrus leaves or fresh mint leaves (optional)	8

Cut each lime in half lengthwise. Remove the pulp from the shells with a melon baller or a small spoon. Transfer the pulp to a sieve set over a bowl, and press down on the pulp with the bottom of a ladle or the back of a wooden spoon to extract all the juice. Discard the pulp and seeds, and reserve the juice. Lightly pare the bottom of the shells to stabilize them. Freeze the lime shells.

Strain 6 tablespoons of the lime juice into a bowl. (Any extra juice may be reserved for another use.) Whisk in the lemon juice, 35 cl (12 fl oz) water, the lime ▶

rind, sugar and egg white, and stir until the sugar has dissolved. Freeze the sorbet, using one of the methods described on page 50.

When the sorbet is firm, pipe or spoon it into the lime shells and return them to the freezer. If you like, garnish each lime shell with a citrus or mint leaf.

EDITOR'S NOTE: *The egg white called for here keeps the sorbet from freezing too hard, making it easier to pipe. An egg white may likewise be added to any citrus sorbet in this section.*

Kiwi Sorbet

Serves 4
Working time: about 15 minutes
Total time: 1 to 3 hours, depending on freezing method

Calories **190**
Protein **2g**
Cholesterol **0mg**
Total fat **1g**
Saturated fat **0g**
Sodium **8mg**

8	kiwi fruits	8
2 tbsp	fresh lemon juice	2 tbsp
100 g	caster sugar	3½ oz

Cut a thin slice from both ends of a kiwi fruit. Stand the fruit on a cutting board. Remove the rest of the skin by slicing vertical strips from the sides of the fruit, taking care not to cut off too much of the flesh. Peel the remaining kiwis the same way.

Quarter each kiwi fruit and put the pieces into a food processor or a blender. Process the kiwis just long enough to purée them without cracking their seeds. Add the lemon juice and sugar, and blend them in.

Freeze the mixture, using one of the methods on page 50. Serve the kiwi sorbet in scoops.

Cranberry Sorbet

Serves 8
Working time: about 15 minutes
Total time: 1 to 3 hours, depending on freezing method

Calories **165**
Protein **0g**
Cholesterol **0mg**
Total fat **0g**
Saturated fat **0g**
Sodium **1mg**

350 g	fresh or frozen cranberries	12 oz
300 g	caster sugar	10 oz
2 tbsp	fresh lemon juice	2 tbsp
1	kiwi fruit (optional), peeled and thinly sliced	1

Put the cranberries into a saucepan with 60 cl (1 pint) of water. Bring the mixture to a simmer and cook it just until the cranberries pop — about 2 minutes. Pass the mixture through a sieve, rubbing the cranberries through with the back of a wooden spoon. Stir in the sugar and lemon juice, then freeze the mixture as described on page 50.

Serve the sorbet in scoops; if you like, garnish each portion with the kiwi slices.

Orange and Passion Fruit Cups

Serves 8
Working time: about 30 minutes
Total time: 1 to 3 hours, depending on freezing method

Calories **160**
Protein **1g**
Cholesterol **0mg**
Total fat **0g**
Saturated fat **0g**
Sodium **4mg**

8	large oranges (about 2 kg/4 lb)	8
4	passion fruit	4
200 g	caster sugar	7 oz

Halve the oranges crosswise, cutting the rind in a zig-zag pattern as demonstrated below. Remove the pulp and seeds from the halves with a melon baller or a small sturdy spoon. Transfer the pulp to a sieve set over a bowl, and press down on the pulp with the bottom of a ladle or the back of a wooden spoon to extract all the juice. Discard the pulp and seeds. Pour 1 litre (1¾ pints) of the orange juice into a bowl. With a small spoon, scrape any remaining pulp from eight of the orange halves to form cups. Freeze these cups; discard the remaining orange shells.

Cut the tops off the passion fruit. Scoop out the pulp and seeds and purée them in a food processor or a blender. Strain the purée into the bowl with the orange juice, then whisk in the sugar. Freeze the mixture, using one of the techniques described on page 50.

When the sorbet is firm, scoop or spoon it into the frozen orange cups. Return the cups to the freezer for about 30 minutes before serving them.

EDITOR'S NOTE: *An equally delicious sorbet results when tangerine juice replaces the orange juice. The dish may also be prepared without the passion fruit, in which case 2 table-spoons of fresh lemon juice should be used in their stead.*

A Zigzag Cut for Fruit Cups

1 *FORMING A FLAT BOTTOM. Holding a citrus fruit (here, an orange) steady, use a small, stainless steel knife to cut a thin slice from its bottom so that the fruit will sit flat when served. (For a lemon, which should be halved lengthwise for greater holding capacity, cut thin slices from two opposite sides to create bases.)*

2 *CUTTING ROUND THE FRUIT. Stand the orange on its flat end. Insert the knife into the midsection at a slant, cutting to the core. Withdraw the knife and make a vertical incision adjacent to the first cut. Alternate slanted and vertical cuts round the orange until the cuts meet.*

3 *SEPARATING THE TOP AND BOTTOM HALVES. To separate the halves, lift off the top; if the halves stick, twist the top and bottom in opposite directions to separate the pieces. Remove the pulp and juice as indicated in the recipe.*

Plum and Red Wine Sorbet with Raisin Sauce

Serves 10
Working time: about 25 minutes
Total time: about 1 day

Calories **180**
Protein **1g**
Cholesterol **0mg**
Total fat **0g**
Saturated fat **0g**
Sodium **3mg**

60 cl	red wine	1 pint
250 g	sugar	8 oz
500 g	ripe red plums, quartered and stoned, two of the quarters sliced for garnish	1 lb
2 tbsp	fresh lemon juice	2 tbsp
45 g	raisins	1½ oz
45 g	sultanas	1½ oz

Combine ½ litre (16 fl oz) of the wine with the sugar in a heavy-bottomed saucepan over medium heat. Bring the mixture to the boil, stirring to dissolve the sugar. When the liquid reaches the boil, reduce the heat, cover the pan, and simmer the syrup for 2 minutes. Stir in the plum quarters; as soon as the syrup returns to a simmer, cover the pan again and cook the plums for 4 minutes more. Strain 12.5 cl (4 fl oz) of the syrup into a small bowl and set it aside for the sauce.

To prepare the sorbet, first purée the plum-wine mixture in a blender or food processor. Blend in the remaining wine and the lemon juice. Let the mixture cool to room temperature, then chill it.

Using one of the methods described on page 50, freeze the sorbet mixture until it is firm but not hard. Transfer the frozen sorbet to a metal mould or bowl. Rap the bottom of the mould or bowl on the counter once or twice to collapse any large air bubbles. Cover the container tightly with plastic film and freeze the sorbet overnight.

To prepare the sauce, combine the reserved 12.5 cl (4 fl oz) of syrup with the raisins and sultanas in a small, heavy-bottomed saucepan. Quickly bring the mixture to the boil, then immediately remove the pan from the heat. Let the sauce cool to room temperature before refrigerating it; the dried fruit will plump up.

Shortly before serving time, unmould the sorbet. Dip the bottom of the mould in hot water for 15 seconds; invert a chilled platter on top and turn both over together. If the dessert does not unmould, wrap it in a towel that has been soaked in hot water. After 15 seconds, remove the towel and lift the mould away. Garnish the sorbet with the reserved plum slices, then cut the sorbet into wedges with a cake slice that has been dipped into hot water. Serve some of the raisin sauce with each portion.

Mint Julep Ice

Serves 8
Working time: about 15 minutes
Total time: 1 to 3 hours, depending on freezing method

Calories **180**
Protein **0g**
Cholesterol **0mg**
Total fat **0g**
Saturated fat **0g**
Sodium **3mg**

250 g	caster sugar	8 oz
60 g	fresh mint leaves plus 2 tbsp chopped fresh mint	2 oz
17.5 cl	bourbon	6 fl oz
2	lemons, juice only	2
8	mint sprigs for garnish	8

In a heavy-bottomed saucepan, combine the sugar, ¾ litre (1¼ pints) of water and the mint leaves. Bring the mixture to the boil over medium heat, stirring to dissolve the sugar. When the mint syrup reaches the boil, cover the pan and boil the syrup for 1 minute. Pour the syrup through a fine sieve into a medium bowl. Allow the syrup to cool to room temperature and then chill it in the refrigerator for about 30 minutes.

When the syrup is cold, combine the 2 tablespoons of chopped mint, the bourbon and the lemon juice in a small bowl. Stir the bourbon mixture into the syrup; freeze the mint julep ice until it is firm, using one of the methods described on page 50.

To serve, scoop the ice into eight sorbet dishes or mint julep cups. Garnish each serving with a sprig of mint.

Gewürztraminer Sorbet with Frosted Grapes

THE WHITE ALSATIAN WINE CALLED FOR IN THIS RECIPE PRODUCES A FULL-FLAVOURED SORBET.

Serves 6
Working time: about 10 minutes
Total time: 1 to 3 hours, depending on freezing method

Calories **225**
Protein **1g**
Cholesterol **0mg**
Total fat **0g**
Saturated fat **0g**
Sodium **11mg**

1	egg white	1
80 g	seedless green grapes	2½ oz
80 g	seedless red grapes	2½ oz
250 g	caster sugar	8 oz
35 cl	Gewürztraminer or Riesling wine	12 fl oz

Whisk together the egg white and ½ tablespoon of water in a bowl. Add all the grapes and stir to coat them with the egg white mixture.

Spread the sugar on a dinner plate. Lift a grape from the egg white and roll it in the sugar, coating it with a generous layer of sugar. Transfer the frosted grape to a clean plate. Coat the remaining grapes the same way, transferring each one to the plate as you finish. To solidify the frosting, let the grapes stand at room temperature while you make the sorbet.

Put ½ litre (16 fl oz) of water and the wine into a bowl, then whisk in the sugar left on the plate. Freeze the sorbet, using one of the methods described on page 50.

Serve the sorbet in scoops, garnishing each portion with a few frosted grapes.

Gin and Pink Grapefruit Sorbet

Serves 6
Working time: about 15 minutes
Total time: 1 to 3 hours, depending on freezing method

Calories **215**
Protein **1g**
Cholesterol **0mg**
Total fat **0g**
Saturated fat **0g**
Sodium **2mg**

1 litre	fresh pink grapefruit juice	1¾ pints
200 g	caster sugar	7 oz
4 tbsp	gin	4 tbsp
1 tbsp	grenadine (optional)	1 tbsp

Combine the grapefruit juice, sugar, gin and grenadine, if you are using it , in a bowl; stir to dissolve the sugar. Freeze the mixture, using one of the methods described on page 50. If you like, present scoops of the sorbet in *tulipes (recipe, page 83)*.

Strawberry and Champagne Sorbet

THE SUCCESS OF THIS RECIPE DEPENDS PARTLY UPON STARTING
OUT WITH CHILLED STRAWBERRIES AND CHAMPAGNE.

Serves 6
Working time: about 15 minutes
Total time: 1 to 2 hours, depending on freezing method

Calories **170**
Protein **0g**
Cholesterol **0mg**
Total fat **0g**
Saturated fat **0g**
Sodium **4mg**

350 g	hulled strawberries, quartered and chilled	12 oz
150 g	caster sugar	5 oz
2 tbsp	fresh lemon juice	2 tbsp
½ litre	chilled dry champagne	16 fl oz
6	strawberries for garnish	6

Put the strawberry quarters, sugar and lemon juice in a food processor or blender; process the mixture briefly so that the berries are finely chopped — not puréed. Add the champagne, pouring it slowly against the inside of the bowl to keep it from frothing. Blend quickly to retain as much effervescence as possible, then freeze the mixture, using one of the methods described on page 50.

Scoop the sorbet into dessert glasses. If you like, garnish each portion with a strawberry and serve with a glass of chilled champagne.

Frozen Peach Yogurt

Serves 6
Working time: about 15 minutes
Total time: 1 to 3 hours, depending on freezing method

Calories **145**
Protein **5g**
Cholesterol **3mg**
Total fat **1g**
Saturated fat **1g**
Sodium **60mg**

750 g	ripe peaches	1 ½ lb
2 tbsp	fresh lemon juice, plus 1 tsp grated lemon rind	2 tbsp
1 tbsp	grated orange rind	1 tbsp
35 cl	plain low-fat yogurt	12 fl oz
2	egg whites	2
125 g	honey	4 oz
3 tbsp	brandy (optional)	3 tbsp

Leaving the peaches unpeeled, halve and stone them. Set one of the peach halves aside. Put the remaining peach halves into a food processor or a blender, together with the lemon juice, lemon rind and orange rind; purée the mixture. Add the yogurt, the egg whites, the honey, and the brandy if you are using it, and blend the mixture for 5 seconds.

Freeze the mixture, following one of the techniques described on page 50.

Before serving, thinly slice the reserved peach half. Scoop the frozen yogurt into dessert glasses or dishes and garnish with the peach slices.

Frozen Vanilla Yogurt

Serves 4
Working time: about 10 minutes
Total time: 1 to 3 hours, depending on freezing method

Calories **165**
Protein **9g**
Cholesterol **9mg**
Total fat **2g**
Saturated fat **2g**
Sodium **125mg**

12.5 cl	semi-skimmed milk	4 fl oz
5 cm	length of vanilla pod, or 1 tsp vanilla extract	2 inch
½ litre	plain low-fat yogurt	16 fl oz
2	egg whites	2
6 tbsp	caster sugar	6 tbsp

If you are using the vanilla pod, warm the milk in a saucepan over low heat. Split the vanilla pod length-wise and add it to the milk. Remove the pan from the heat and let the vanilla pod steep until the milk has cooled to room temperature — about 15 minutes.

Remove the pod from the milk and scrape the seeds inside it into the milk. If you are using vanilla extract, simply combine it with the unheated milk.

Whisk the yogurt, egg whites and sugar into the milk. Freeze the mixture using one of the methods described on page 50.

Frozen Raspberry Yogurt

Serves 6
Working time: about 15 minutes
Total time: 1 to 3 hours, depending on freezing method

Calories **140**
Protein **5g**
Cholesterol **5mg**
Total fat **1g**
Saturated fat **1g**
Sodium **70mg**

300 g	fresh or frozen raspberries, thawed	10 oz
½ litre	plain low-fat yogurt	16 fl oz
100 g	caster sugar	3 ½ oz
2	egg whites	2
4 tbsp	crème de cassis (optional)	4 tbsp

Purée the raspberries in a food processor or a blender. Then, to remove the raspberry seeds, pass the purée through a fine sieve into a bowl; use a spatula to force the purée through the wire mesh. Combine the purée with the yogurt and sugar, whisk in the egg whites, then freeze the mixture using one of the methods described on page 50.

Pass the crème de cassis separately so that each diner can pour a little over the yogurt.

EDITOR'S NOTE: *If desired, two yogurts can be swirled together. Make frozen vanilla yogurt (recipe above). Spoon the frozen raspberry yogurt inside a piping bag, keeping it to one side; spoon the frozen vanilla yogurt on top of the raspberry yogurt, filling the other side of the bag. Pipe out the two yogurts together in a mounting spiral.*

Frozen Banana Yogurt with Streusel Crumbs

Serves 8
Working time: about 15 minutes
Total time: 1 to 3 hours, depending on freezing method

Calories **190**
Protein **6g**
Cholesterol **8mg**
Total fat **3g**
Saturated fat **2g**
Sodium **100mg**

350 g	ripe bananas	12 oz
2 tbsp	fresh lemon juice	2 tbsp
½ litre	plain low-fat yogurt	16 fl oz
2	egg whites, at room temperature	2
6 tbsp	caster sugar	6 tbsp
3	slices wholemeal bread	3
15 g	unsalted butter	½ oz
4 tbsp	light brown sugar	4 tbsp
1 tbsp	finely chopped walnuts	1 tbsp

Purée the bananas and lemon juice in a food processor or a blender. Add the yogurt, egg whites and caster sugar, and blend the mixture for 5 seconds.

Freeze the yogurt mixture, using one of the methods described on page 50.

While the yogurt mixture is freezing, make the streusel: preheat the oven to 170°C (325°F or Mark 3). Tear each slice of bread into three or four pieces; put the bread pieces in a food processor or a blender and process them until they are reduced to fine crumbs. Spread the crumbs in a baking tin and bake them, stirring once or twice to ensure even cooking, until they are crisp — about 15 minutes. Cut the butter into small bits and scatter them over the breadcrumbs. Return the pan to the oven just long enough to melt the butter — about 1 minute. Stir the breadcrumbs to coat them with the butter, then transfer the mixture to a bowl. Stir in the brown sugar and walnuts, and set the mixture aside.

When the yogurt mixture is nearly frozen — it will still be soft — stir in all but 2 tablespoons of the streusel mixture. Return the yogurt to the freezer for approximately 15 minutes more to firm it up. Just before serving the yogurt, sprinkle the reserved streusel over the top.

Iced Apple Mousse Cake with Brandy Snaps

THE RECIPE FOR THE BRANDY SNAPS PICTURED HERE
APPEARS ON PAGE 81.

Serves 12
Working time: about 1 hour
Total time: 2½ to 4 hours, depending
on freezing method

Calories **175**
Protein **2g**
Cholesterol **10mg**
Total fat **4g**
Saturated fat **2g**
Sodium **30mg**

1 kg	crisp eating apples	2 lb
4 tbsp	fresh lemon juice	4 tbsp
½ tsp	ground cloves	½ tsp
½ tsp	ground cinnamon	½ tsp
30 g	unsalted butter	1 oz
100 g	caster sugar	3½ oz
6	egg whites	6
12	tuile brandy snaps	12
Apple fans		
2	crisp eating apples	2
2 tsp	honey	2 tsp

To make the apple mousse, peel and core the 1 kg (2 lb) of apples, then cut them into 1 cm (½ inch) chunks. Toss the apples with the lemon juice, cloves and cinnamon.

Melt the butter in a large, heavy frying pan over medium heat. Add the apple mixture and cook it, stir-ring frequently, for about 10 minutes. Sprinkle in the sugar and continue to cook the mixture stirring often, for 5 minutes more.

Put the apple mixture into a food processor or a blender and process it until it is very smooth, stopping at least once to scrape down the sides. Transfer the mixture to a shallow bowl and whisk in the egg whites. Freeze the mixture, using one of the methods described on page 50.

Preheat the oven to 180°C (350°F or Mark 4).

To prepare the apple fans, peel the remaining two apples and cut them in half lengthwise. Remove the cores, then slice the apple halves thinly, keeping the slices together. Fan out each sliced apple half on a bak-ing sheet. Dribble the honey over the apple fans and bake them until they are tender — about 15 minutes. Allow the fans to cool to room temperature, then refrigerate them.

Transfer the apple mousse to a 23 cm (9 inch) spring-form tin and freeze it until it is solid — about 1 hour.

To unmould the cake, run a knife round the inside of the tin, then place a hot, damp towel on the bottom for about 10 seconds. Invert a plate on the cake; turn both cake and plate over together. Remove the sides of the tin, and smooth the surface of the cake with a long knife or spatula.

Arrange the chilled apple fans on top of the cake; decorate the sides of the cake with the brandy snaps.

Two-Melon Ice
with Poppy Seeds
and Port Sauce

Calories **183**
Protein **2g**
Cholesterol **0mg**
Total fat **1g**
Saturated fat **0g**
Sodium **20mg**

Port sauce:
Calories **65**
Protein **0g**
Cholesterol **0mg**
Total fat **0g**
Saturated fat **0g**
Sodium **2mg**

Serves 8
Working time: about 15 minutes
Total time: 1 to 3 hours, depending on freezing method

1	ripe honeydew melon (about 2.5 kg/5 lb)	1
1	ripe cantaloupe melon (about 1.5 kg/3 lb)	1
1 tsp	poppy seeds	1 tsp
⅛ tsp	ground mace	⅛ tsp
4 tbsp	fresh lemon juice	4 tbsp
200 to 275 g	caster sugar, depending on the sweetness of the melon	7 to 9 oz
Port sauce (optional)		
35 cl	ruby port	12 fl oz
2 tsp	cornflour	2 tsp

With a narrow-bladed knife, halve the honeydew melon crosswise, using a zigzag cut to produce a saw-tooth pattern in the rind. Remove and discard the seeds. Select the more attractive half of the melon for serving; with a melon baller, scoop from it balls of flesh. Refrigerate the melon balls in a large bowl. Cut some of the flesh from the other melon half and purée it in a food processor or a blender — there should be about ½ litre (16 fl oz) of purée. If the purée measures less than ½ litre (16 fl oz), process more melon flesh; if it measures more, reserve the excess for another use. Refrigerate the purée.

Slice the cantaloupe in half with a simple cross-wise cut. Scoop out one half into balls and refrigerate them with the honeydew balls until serving time. Cut the remaining cantaloupe half into chunks and purée the chunks to produce ½ litre (16 fl oz) of purée. Stir the cantaloupe and honeydew purées together and chill them.

Discard all the melon shells except the honeydew half you selected for serving. Scrape the inside of the shell clean. Pare a thin slice from the bottom so that the melon will stand upright, then freeze the shell.

Combine the chilled melon purée with the poppy seeds, mace, lemon juice and sugar. Freeze the mixture, using one of the methods described on page 50.

To make the sauce, bring 30 cl (½ pint) of the port to the boil in a saucepan. Combine the remaining port with the cornflour and stir the mixture into the boiling port. Cook the sauce, stirring constantly, until it thickens — about 1 minute. Allow the sauce to cool to room temperature, then chill it.

Use an ice-cream scoop to fill the frozen honeydew shell with balls of the melon ice. Scatter the chilled melon balls over the top and pass the sauce separately.

Cappuccino Parfaits

Serves 8
Working time: about 35 minutes
Total time: 1 to 3 hours, depending on freezing method

Calories **130**
Protein **1g**
Cholesterol **11mg**
Total fat **3g**
Saturated fat **2g**
Sodium **16mg**

1	orange, pared rind only	1
2 tbsp	high-roast instant coffee powder	2 tbsp
200 g	caster sugar	7 oz
4 tbsp	double cream	4 tbsp
½ tsp	ground cinnamon	½ tsp
2	egg whites	2
	cocoa powder	

In a heatproof bowl, combine the orange rind, instant coffee powder, 150 g (5 oz) of the sugar and ½ litre (16 fl oz) of boiling water. Stir to dissolve the sugar, then let the orange rind steep for 10 minutes. Remove the rind and discard it. Using one of the techniques described on page 50, freeze the coffee mixture.

When the mixture is frozen, divide it among eight glass coffee cups or glasses; freeze the containers.

In a small bowl, whip together the cream and cinnamon until soft peaks form; set the mixture aside. In another bowl, beat the egg whites until they can hold soft peaks when the beater is lifted from the bowl. Continue beating, gradually adding the remaining sugar, until the whites are glossy and form stiff peaks. Fold the whipped cream into the egg whites. Fill each of the cups or glasses with some of the egg white-cream mixture. Freeze the parfaits until they are firm —about 30 minutes.

Just before serving the parfaits, dust each one with some cocoa powder.

Frozen Piña Coladas

Serves 8
Working time: about 20 minutes
Total time: about 2 hours and 20 minutes

Calories **125**
Protein **3g**
Cholesterol **2mg**
Total fat **2g**
Saturated fat **1g**
Sodium **80mg**

75 g	fresh pineapple flesh, chopped	2½ oz
75 g	peeled banana, chopped	2½ oz
½ litre	buttermilk	16 fl oz
100 g	caster sugar	3½ oz
2	egg whites	2
4 tbsp	dark rum	4 tbsp
3 tbsp	shredded coconut for garnish	3 tbsp

Process the pineapple and the banana in a blender or a food processor, stopping once to scrape down the sides with a rubber spatula, until every trace of fibre has disappeared and a smooth purée results — about 1 minute. (There should be approximately ¼ litre/8 fl oz of purée.) Blend in the buttermilk, sugar, egg whites and rum. Freeze the mixture, using one of the methods described on page 50.

Scoop the sorbet into glasses and keep in the freezer until serving time.

To toast the coconut, spread it in a baking tin and set it in a preheated 180°C (350°F or Mark 4) oven. Toast the coconut, stirring every 5 minutes, until it is lightly browned — 15 to 20 minutes.

Just before serving the desserts, sprinkle some of the toasted coconut over each one.

Sliced Watermelon Sorbet

Serves 16
Working time: about 20 minutes
Total time: 4 to 6 hours (includes chilling)

Calories **90**	1	watermelon (about 3.5 kg/8 lb)	1
Protein **1g**	200 g	caster sugar	7 oz
Cholesterol **0mg**	2½ tbsp	fresh lemon juice	2½ tbsp
Total fat **1g**	145 g	fresh blueberries	5 oz
Saturated fat **0g**			
Sodium **3mg**			

Halve the watermelon lengthwise. Scoop out all the flesh and put it into a large bowl. Select the more attractive half of the watermelon to use for serving; discard the other half. Cut the watermelon half crosswise into slices about 2.5 cm (1 inch) thick. Reassemble the slices so that the watermelon shell appears intact, and freeze it until it is rock-hard and the slices are firmly stuck together. (In order for the slices to cohere, it may be necessary to prop the shell in place during freezing.)

Purée the watermelon flesh in several batches in a blender or food processor, then press it through a sieve to filter out the seeds. Measure the strained fruit; there should be about 1.75 litres (3 pints). (If you have more or less fruit, increase or decrease the amount of sugar accordingly by 2 tablespoons per ¼ litre/8 fl oz of fruit.) Stir the sugar and lemon juice into the strained fruit, then freeze the mixture using one of the methods on page 50. No matter which freezing method you select, do not stir the blueberries into the watermelon sorbet until the end of its freezing period.

When the melon shell is frozen solid, fill it with the blueberry-studded sorbet, smoothing the top so the final result will resemble a freshly cut watermelon half. Freeze the assembly until it is solid throughout — at least 2 hours.

Present the watermelon intact. Using the precut lines as a guide, cut the watermelon into slices.

Frozen Lemon Meringue Torte

Serves 8
Working time: about 1 hour and 15 minutes
Total time: 1½ to 4 hours, depending on freezing method

Calories **240**
Protein **4g**
Cholesterol **0mg**
Total fat **5g**
Saturated fat **0g**
Sodium **30mg**

8	lemons	8
250 g	caster sugar	8 oz
2	egg whites	2
2 tbsp	cocoa powder	2 tbsp
Almond meringues		
2	egg whites	2
6 tbsp	caster sugar	6 tbsp
75 g	blanched almonds, ground	2½ oz
2 tbsp	icing sugar	2 tbsp

Grate the rind from three of the lemons and put it into a blender or a food processor. Working over a bowl to catch the juice, peel and segment one of the lemons as shown on page 14. Squeeze the pulpy core of membranes over the bowl to extract every bit of juice. Repeat the process with the remaining lemons. To remove the seeds, strain the lemon juice into the blender or food processor. Add the lemon segments, the sugar, egg whites and 55 cl (18 fl oz) of water to the rind and juice, and purée the mixture.

Freeze the lemon mixture following one of the methods described on page 50. While the mixture is freezing, make the almond meringues.

Preheat the oven to 110°C (200°F or Mark ¼). Line a baking sheet with greaseproof paper, or butter the sheet lightly and then dust it with flour.

Beat the two egg whites until they form soft peaks. Beat in the sugar a tablespoon at a time; when all the sugar has been incorporated, continue beating the whites until they are glossy and hold stiff peaks, sprinkle the ground almonds over the beaten whites and fold them in.

Fit a piping bag with a 1 cm (½ inch) plain nozzle and spoon the meringue into the bag. Pipe the meringue on to the prepared baking sheet in strips nearly the length of the sheet; the strips should be about 2.5 cm (1 inch) wide and 2.5 cm (1 inch) apart. (If you have no piping bag, shape the strips with a spoon.) Sprinkle the strips evenly with the icing sugar, then bake them for 1 hour.

Turn off the oven and let the strips dry, with the oven door ajar, for another hour; if necessary, use a wooden spoon to prop the oven door open. Remove the baking sheet from the oven and gently loosen the meringues. Break the meringues into bars about 7.5 cm (3 inches) long; when they have cooled, store them in an airtight container until you are ready to decorate the torte.

When the lemon sorbet is frozen, transfer it to a 20 or 23 cm (8 or 9 inch) springform tin. Use a rubber spatula to distribute the sorbet evenly in the tin. Rap the bottom of the tin on the work surface to collapse any large air bubbles, then smooth the top of the sorbet with the spatula. Freeze the torte until it is firm — about 1 hour.

Remove the sides of the springform tin. Slide a knife or a long metal spatula between the torte and the base of the tin, and transfer the torte to a serving platter. Smooth the sides of the torte with a knife dipped in hot water. Press the meringue bars in place in a random pattern over the top and on the sides of the torte. (The torte can be kept in the freezer with the meringue bars attached.)

Just before serving, dust the torte with the cocoa powder: put the cocoa into a sieve, then tap the sieve gently as you move it over the torte.

Frozen Nectarine and Plum Terrine

Serves 10
Working time: about 45 minutes
Total time: about 1 day (includes freezing)

Calories **190**
Protein **1g**
Cholesterol **0mg**
Total fat **1g**
Saturated fat **0g**
Sodium **1mg**

Nectarine sorbet		
500 g	nectarines, halved and stoned	1 lb
12.5 cl	fresh orange juice	4 fl oz
4 tbsp	fresh lemon juice	4 tbsp
150 g	caster sugar	5 oz
Plum sorbet		
500 g	plums, halved and stoned	1 lb
17.5 cl	fresh orange juice	6 fl oz
150 g	caster sugar	5 oz
Garnish		
1	nectarine, halved, stoned and sliced into thin wedges	1
2	plums, halved, stoned and sliced into thin wedges	2

To prepare the nectarine sorbet, purée the nectarines, orange juice, lemon juice and sugar in a food processor or blender. Transfer the purée to a freezer container and freeze it, using one of the methods described on page 50. Prepare the plum sorbet in the same way and freeze it as well.

When both sorbets are firm but not hard, line a 1.5 litre (2½ pint) loaf tin or metal mould with plastic film.

Put half the nectarine sorbet into the lined tin, smoothing it out with a rubber spatula. Top the nectarine sorbet with half of the plum sorbet; smooth its top the same way. Repeat the layering process with the remaining sorbet to make four layers in all. To collapse any air bubbles, tap the bottom of the tin on the work surface. Cover the top of the sorbet with plastic film and freeze the terrine overnight.

Remove the plastic film from the top. Invert the terrine on to a chilled platter. Unwrap the terrine and cut it into 1 cm (½ inch) slices, dipping the knife into hot water and wiping it off between slices. Garnish the slices with the wedges of nectarine and plum.

Grape Lollies

THESE FROZEN CONFECTIONS ARE FORMED
IN A MADELEINE TRAY.

Makes 12
Working time: about 30 minutes
Total time: about 1 hour and 20 minutes

Calories **70**
Protein **0g**
Cholesterol **0mg**
Total fat **0g**
Saturated fat **0g**
Sodium **2mg**

500 g	seedless green grapes	1 lb
500 g	seedless black grapes	1 lb
5 tbsp	caster sugar	5 tbsp

Purée the green grapes in a food processor or a blender. Strain the purée through a fine sieve into a small saucepan. Bring the purée to a simmer over medium-high heat, then stir in 2½ tablespoons of the sugar, and remove the pan from the heat. When the mixture has cooled to room temperature, pour it into a 12-space madeleine tray, filling each space to the brim. Reserve the excess purée. Chill the tray in the freezer until the purée has nearly set — about 30 minutes.

Lay the end of a flat ice lolly stick in the centre of each of the six frozen sorbets in the bottom row of the tray; the sticks should overhang the tray's bottom edge. Return the tray to the freezer.

While the tray is chilling, purée the black grapes in a food processor or blender and strain the purée into the saucepan. Bring the purée to a simmer over medium-high heat, then stir in the remaining 2½ tablespoons of sugar, and remove the pan from the heat. Pour the mixture into a bowl and set it aside to cool.

When the green-grape mixture has frozen solid, remove the madeleine tray from the freezer; pop out the sorbets in the top row and brush their flat sides with the reserved green-grape mixture. Set one of the painted sorbets on top of a sorbet that is still in the tray, and press it in place. Repeat the process to form six lollies in all, then return the tray to the freezer for 30 minutes.

When the green-grape lollies have frozen solid, remove them from the tray mould and return them to the freezer. Clean the mould and use it to make six black-grape lollies, using the same method.

EDITOR'S NOTE: *Wooden or plastic ice lolly sticks are sold at newsagents and kitchen shops.*

Mango Ice Cream

Serves 8
Working time: about 40 minutes
Total time: 1 to 3 hours, depending on freezing method

Calories **155**			
Protein **3g**	1.5 kg	ripe mangoes, peeled and	3 lb
Cholesterol **18mg**		stoned (page 29)	
Total fat **5g**	35 cl	semi-skimmed milk	12 fl oz
Saturated fat **3g**	6 tbsp	double cream	6 tbsp
Sodium **35mg**	3 tbsp	caster sugar	3 tbsp
	1	lime, juice only	1

Cut enough of the mangoes into small cubes to weigh 250 g (8 oz); chill the cubes in the refrigerator.

Purée the remaining mangoes in a blender or a food processor and transfer the purée to a bowl. (There should be about ½ litre/16 fl oz of purée.) Add the milk, cream, sugar and lime juice, and stir until the sugar dissolves. Freeze the ice cream, using one of the methods described on page 50.

Scoop the ice cream into serving dishes, then serve each portion with some of the chilled mango cubes.

The five ice cream recipes that follow contain no double cream, yet each is a delightfully smooth dessert.

Spiced Coffee Ice Cream

Serves 8
Working time: about 15 minutes
Total time: 1 to 3 hours, depending on freezing method

Calories **160**
Protein **6g**
Cholesterol **15mg**
Total fat **5g**
Saturated fat **3g**
Sodium **70mg**

325 g	low-fat ricotta cheese	11 oz
12.5 cl	plain low-fat yogurt	4 fl oz
135 g	caster sugar	4½ oz
¼ litre	freshly brewed triple-strength coffee, strained and chilled	8 fl oz
½ tsp	ground cinnamon	½ tsp
½ tsp	ground cardamom, or ¼ tsp grated nutmeg	½ tsp
½ tsp	pure vanilla extract	½ tsp
30 g	plain chocolate, grated	1 oz

Purée the ricotta, yogurt and sugar in a food processor or a blender, stopping at least once to scrape down the sides, until you have a very smooth purée. Whisk the coffee, cinnamon, cardamom or nutmeg, vanilla and chocolate into the purée. Freeze, using one of the techniques on page 50. If using the food processor method, add the chocolate after processing the mixture.

Strawberry Ice Cream

Serves 8
Working time: about 30 minutes
Total time: 1 to 3 hours, depending on freezing method

Calories **155**
Protein **7g**
Cholesterol **15mg**
Total fat **4g**
Saturated fat **2g**
Sodium **80mg**

750 g	ripe strawberries, hulled	1 ½ lb
100 g	caster sugar	3 ½ oz
1 ½ tbsp	fresh lemon juice	1 ½ tbsp
2 tbsp	Grand Marnier, or 1 tbsp grated orange rind	2 tbsp
350 g	low-fat ricotta cheese	12 oz
12.5 cl	plain low-fat yogurt	4 fl oz
2	egg whites	2

In a food processor or a blender, purée the strawberries with the sugar, lemon juice and the Grand Marnier or orange rind. Transfer the purée to a large bowl and set it aside.

Rinse out the food processor or blender. Add the ricotta cheese and the yogurt and purée them, stopping at least once to scrape down the sides, until you have a very smooth purée. Whisk the ricotta-yogurt purée and the egg whites into the strawberry purée, then freeze the mixture, using one of the methods described on page 50.

Peach Ice Cream

Serves 8
Working time: about 30 minutes
Total time: 1 to 3 hours, depending on freezing method

Calories **195**
Protein **8g**
Cholesterol **18mg**
Total fat **5g**
Saturated fat **3g**
Sodium **95mg**

1 kg	ripe peaches	2 lb
1½ tbsp	fresh lemon juice	1½ tbsp
350 g	low-fat ricotta cheese	12 oz
12.5 cl	plain low-fat yogurt	4 fl oz
2 tbsp	soured cream	2 tbsp
12.5 cl	semi-skimmed milk	4 fl oz
75 g	light brown sugar	2½ oz
2	egg whites	2
½ tsp	pure vanilla extract	½ tsp
¼ tsp	almond extract	¼ tsp

Bring 2 litres (3½ pints) of water to the boil in a large saucepan. Add the peaches and blanch them until their skins loosen — 30 seconds to 1 minute. Remove the peaches with a slotted spoon and set them aside; when they are cool enough to handle, peel them, cut them in half and remove their stones.

Cut enough of the peach halves into 1 cm (½ inch) dice to weigh about 375 g (13 oz). Purée the remaining peach halves with the lemon juice in a food processor or a blender. Transfer the peach purée to a large bowl and set it aside.

Put the ricotta, yogurt and soured cream in the food processor or blender; purée the mixture until it has a creamy consistency, stopping at least once to scrape down the sides. Blend in the milk, brown sugar, egg whites, and the vanilla and almond extracts, then whisk the mixture into the peach purée.

Stir the reserved peach dice into the purée and freeze it, using one of the methods described on page 50. If you use the food processor method of freezing, do not add the peach dice until after you have processed the ice cream.

Ginger-Date Ice Cream

THE CREAMY TEXTURE OF THIS LOW-FAT ICE CREAM
COMES FROM THE PAIRING OF RICOTTA CHEESE AND YOGURT.

Serves 8
Working time: about 25 minutes
Total time: 1 to 3 hours, depending on freezing method

Calories **120**
Protein **6g**
Cholesterol **12mg**
Total fat **3g**
Saturated fat **2g**
Sodium **75mg**

¼ litre	semi-skimmed milk	8 fl oz
125 g	dried stoned dates, cut into small pieces	4 oz
6 tbsp	plain low-fat yogurt	6 tbsp
250 g	low-fat ricotta cheese	8 oz
2 tbsp	caster sugar	2 tbsp
2	egg whites	2
1 tbsp	finely chopped crystallized ginger	1 tbsp
½ tbsp	fresh lemon juice	½ tbsp

Warm the milk in a saucepan over very low heat. Remove the pan from the heat and add all but 2 table-spoons of the dates; steep the dates for 10 minutes.

Purée the date-milk mixture in a food processor or a blender, then transfer the purée to a large bowl.

Purée the yogurt, ricotta cheese and sugar in the food processor or blender, stopping at least once to scrape down the sides, until you have a very smooth purée. Add the yogurt-ricotta purée to the date-milk purée in the bowl, and whisk the two together. Refrigerate the bowl for 15 minutes.

Blend the egg whites into the refrigerated purée, then freeze the mixture using one of the techniques described on page 50. If you plan to use an ice cream maker, stir the crystallized ginger, lemon juice and reserved 2 tablespoons of dates into the mixture before freezing it. If you are using the hand-whisking method, stir in the lemon juice, ginger and reserved dates when the mixture is almost solid. For the food processor method, add the lemon juice during the processing, then blend in the ginger and reserved dates.

Cherry Ice Cream

Serves 8
Working time: about 30 minutes
Total time: 1 to 3 hours, depending on freezing method

Calories **180**
Protein **8g**
Cholesterol **16mg**
Total fat **6g**
Saturated fat **3g**
Sodium **90mg**

350 g	sweet cherries	12 o
100 g	sugar	3½ o
350 g	low-fat ricotta cheese	12 o
12.5 cl	plain low-fat yogurt	4 fl o
½ tsp	almond extract	½ ts
½ tsp	pure vanilla extract	½ ts
12.5 cl	semi-skimmed milk	4 fl o
2 tbsp	toasted almonds, crushed	2 tbs
2	egg whites	

Stone and quarter the cherries, working over a larg
bowl to catch any juice *(page 24)*. Put the stoned cher
ries, the sugar and 12.5 cl (4 fl oz) of water in a heavy
bottomed saucepan. Bring the liquid to the boil ove
medium-high heat, then reduce the heat and simme
the cherries for 10 minutes.

Remove the cherries from the syrup with a slotte
spoon and continue cooking the syrup until it i
reduced by one half — about 5 minutes. Refrigerat
the cherries and half of the syrup.

Put the ricotta, yogurt, almond extract and vanill
extract into a food processor or a blender. Purée th
mixture, stopping at least once to scrape down th
sides, until you have a very smooth purée. Stir the cher
ries and the syrup into the ricotta mixture, then add th
milk, almonds and egg whites, and mix well. Freeze th
mixture, using one of the techniques described o
page 50. If you are using the food processor method
do not add the cherries and almonds until after yo
have processed the mixture.

Avocado and Grapefruit Bombe with Candied Rind

THIS ELEGANT PRESENTATION OF GRAPEFRUIT SORBET
AND AVOCADO ICE MILK MAKES AN ELABORATE BUT PERFECT
ENDING TO A SPECIAL MEAL.

Serves 12
Working time: about 1 hour
Total time: 2 to 4 hours, depending on freezing method

Calories **265**
Protein **3g**
Cholesterol **4mg**
Total fat **9g**
Saturated fat **2g**
Sodium **30mg**

Grapefruit sorbet		
4	large grapefruits	
300 g	caster sugar	10 o
Avocado ice milk		
2	large ripe avocados	
¼ litre	whole milk	8 fl o
¼ litre	semi-skimmed milk	8 fl o
100 g	caster sugar	3½ o
2 tbsp	finely chopped crystallized ginger	2 tbs

Put a 1.5 litre (2½ pint) round mould into the freeze
Using a vegetable peeler or a paring knife, pare th

rind from two of the grapefruits. Cook the rind in a saucepan of boiling water for 10 minutes, then drain it. Julienne half of the rind and crystallize it *(recipe, right).* Set the candied rind aside. Put the uncandied rind into a food processor or a blender.

Remove the pith from the two pared grapefruits and discard it. Cut away all of the peel from the remaining two grapefruits and discard it too. Working over a bowl to catch the juice, cut between the membranes of the grapefruits to free the segments *(page 14).* Discard the seeds. Transfer the juice and the segments to the food processor or blender, and purée them with the uncandied rind. Add the sugar and process until it is dissolved. Freeze the grapefruit sorbet, using one of the methods described on page 50.

Remove the mould from the freezer and line it evenly with the sorbet, leaving a large hollow in the centre for the avocado mixture. Return the mould to the freezer.

Peel and stone the avocados, and purée their flesh. Blend in the whole milk, semi-skimmed milk and sugar. Freeze, using one of the methods on page 50. Mix in the ginger half way through the freezing process.

When the ice milk is frozen, spoon it into the hollow in the grapefruit sorbet. Then freeze the mould for 1½ hours. Before serving, dip the bottom of the mould in hot water, then invert a chilled platter over the top and turn the two over together. Lift the mould away. Garnish the bombe with the candied grapefruit rind, and serve immediately.

Candied Citrus Rind

Makes about 60 g (2 oz)
Working time: about 20 minutes
Total time: about 35 minutes

| 45 g | julienned citrus rind (orange, grapefruit, lemon or lime) | 1½ oz |
| 4 tbsp | caster sugar | 4 tbsp |

Per tablespoon:
Calories **16**
Protein **0g**
Cholesterol **0mg**
Total fat **0g**
Saturated fat **0g**
Sodium **0mg**

Put the citrus rind into a saucepan with ¼ litre (8 fl oz) of water and bring the water to the boil. Cook the rind for 15 minutes, then remove it with a slotted spoon, and spread it on paper towels to drain. Pour the water out of the saucepan. Add the sugar, 2 tablespoons of cold water and the drained rind to the pan. Cook the mixture over high heat, stirring constantly, until the rind is coated with white, crystallized sugar — about 3 minutes. Remove the rind from the pan and set it on greaseproof paper to dry.

EDITOR'S NOTE: *Candied rind may be stored in an airtight container at room temperature for up to a week.*

Amaretti

SERVE THESE ALMOND BISCUITS AS AN ACCOMPANIMENT TO
CREAMY DESSERTS AND SORBETS, OR ON THEIR OWN
WITH YOUR FAVOURITE AFTER-DINNER BEVERAGE.

Makes about 100 biscuits
Working time: about 30 minutes
Total time: about 9 hours (includes standing time)

Per biscuit:
Calories **20**
Protein **0g**
Cholesterol **0mg**
Total fat **1g**
Saturated fat **0g**
Sodium **9mg**

250 g	almond paste	8 oz
2 tsp	pure almond extract	2 tsp
200 g	caster sugar	7 oz
4	egg whites	4
⅛ tsp	salt	⅛ tsp
	icing sugar	

Mix together the almond paste, almond extract and 135 g (4½ oz) of the sugar in a bowl. Beating continuously, gradually add about half of the egg whites. Continue beating until the mixture has lightened in texture and colour — about 3 minutes.

To prepare the meringue, beat the remaining egg whites in a bowl until they are foamy. Add the salt, then continue beating the whites until they form soft peaks. Gradually add the remaining sugar, beating all the while, until the whites form stiff peaks.

Fold one third of the meringue into the almond mixture to lighten it, then fold in the remaining meringue. Spoon the mixture into a piping bag fitted with a plain nozzle. Line two baking sheets with non-stick parchment paper and pipe out the mixture in mounds about 2.5 cm (1 inch) across. Sprinkle the mounds generously with icing sugar and let them stand at room temperature for at least 8 hours.

Preheat the oven to 180°C (350°F or Mark 4).

To allow the amaretti to puff during baking, pinch a mound at its base, cracking the surface. Pinch the mound once more to crack its surface a second time at a right angle to the first. Repeat the process to crack all the amaretti.

Bake the amaretti, with the oven door propped slightly ajar with the handle of a wooden spoon, for 30 minutes. Remove the biscuits from the oven and let them stand, still on the paper, until they have cooled to room temperature. Remove the amaretti from the parchment paper, and store them in an airtight container until serving time.

EDITOR'S NOTE: *The almond paste called for in this recipe is available in supermarkets.*

Tuile Brandy Snaps

THESE BISCUITS ARE DESIGNED TO DECORATE THE
APPLE MOUSSE CAKE ON PAGE 65. THEY ALSO MAKE A
DELIGHTFUL DESSERT WHEN SERVED ON THEIR OWN.

Makes 12 biscuits
Working time: about 10 minutes
Total time: about 20 minutes

Per biscuit:
Calories **54**
Protein **0g**
Cholesterol **5mg**
Total fat **2g**
Saturated fat **1g**
Sodium **3mg**

30 g	unsalted butter	1 oz
2 tbsp	sugar	2 tbsp
2 tbsp	golden syrup	2 tbsp
1 tsp	molasses	1 tsp
1 tsp	ground ginger	1 tsp
½ tsp	grated lemon rind	½ tsp
2 tbsp	brandy	2 tbsp
45 g	plain flour	1½ oz

Preheat the oven to 200°C (400°F or Mark 6).

Put the butter, sugar, syrup, molasses, ginger, rind and brandy into a small saucepan and bring the mixture to the boil. Cook the mixture for 1 minute, then remove it from the heat and let it cool for 1 minute.

Add the flour and whisk the batter until it is smooth.

Lightly oil a heavy baking sheet. Drop the batter on to the sheet in heaped teaspoonfuls at least 7.5 cm (3 inches) apart. (It may be necessary to bake the biscuits in two batches; if you are using two baking sheets, stagger the cooking to allow enough time to shape the biscuits after they are baked.) Bake the biscuits until they turn slightly darker — 3 to 4 minutes.

Remove the baking sheet from the oven and let it sit for 1 minute while the biscuits firm up a little. With a metal spatula, remove some of the still-soft biscuits and drape them over a clean rolling pin to cool. Remove the curved biscuits from the rolling pin as soon as they harden — about 30 seconds. Immediately repeat the procedure to fashion the remaining biscuits. If any of the biscuits become hard while they are still on the baking sheet, return them to the oven for a few seconds to soften them.

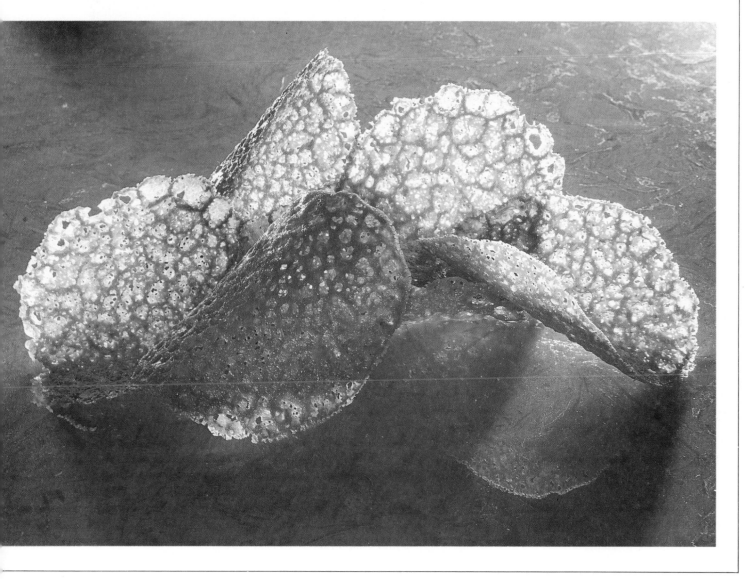

Shaping Tulipes

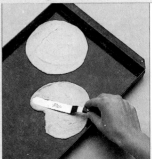

1 SPREADING THE BATTER.
Drop a heaped tablespoon of batter on to a prepared baking sheet. With a palette knife or back of a spoon, spread in a circular motion to produce discs 15 to 18 cm (6 to 7 inches) across. Place two more biscuits on the sheet, and bake as directed (opposite).

2 MOULDING THE CUPS.
Working rapidly, lift a biscuit from the sheet with a metal spatula and place it over the bottom of an overturned drinking glass. Gently press down the biscuit's sides with your fingers to form a tulip-like cup. Let the biscuit firm up before removing it. Set it aside and proceed to the next tulipe.

Rolling "Cigarettes"

1 SPREADING THE BATTER.
Drop a scant tablespoon of batter on to a prepared baking sheet. With the back of a soup spoon, or palette knife, spread out the batter in a circular motion, to produce discs 7.5 to 10 cm (3 to 4 inches) across. Repeat the process until the sheet is full, and bake as directed (opposite).

2 ROLLING THE BISCUITS.
Working rapidly, lift a baked biscuit from the sheet with a metal spatula and roll it around a wooden spoon handle or a pencil. When the biscuit has firmed up, slide it off and set it aside. Repeat the procedure to form the other cigarettes.

Stencilling Leaves

1 *FILLING THE STENCIL. Place a biscuit stencil at the corner of a prepared baking sheet and drop a spoonful of batter into the opening. Holding the stencil steady, use a palette knife or metal spatula to spread the batter in an even layer within the opening. Lift the stencil straight up. Repeat the procedure until biscuit leaves fill the baking sheet.*

2 *DECORATING THE LEAVES. Dip the tip of a small spoon or knife into the chocolate batter prepared according to the recipe (right). Using the spoon or knife like a pen, draw veins on the leaves. Bake and shape the biscuits as indicated in the recipe.*

Shaped Biscuits

THIS BISCUIT DOUGH CAN BE FASHIONED INTO
THE FANCIFUL SHAPES ON THE LEFT. IT YIELDS ABOUT
12 *TULIPES*, 16 OAK LEAVES OR 18 CIGARETTES.

Working (and total) time: about 40 minutes

60 g	unsalted butter, at room temperature	2 oz
60 g	icing sugar, sifted	2 oz
½ tsp	pure vanilla extract	½ tsp
2 tsp	grated grapefruit, orange or lemon rind (optional)	2 tsp
2	egg whites, at room temperature	2
45 g	plain flour	1½ oz
½ tsp	cocoa powder	½ tsp

Lightly oil a baking sheet or line it with non-stick parchment paper. Preheat the oven to 190°C (375°F or Mark 5). In a large bowl, beat together the butter, sugar, vanilla and the citrus rind, if you are using it. Stir in a little of the egg white. Continue adding the egg white a little at a time, mixing in about 2 tablespoons of the flour after each addition of egg white. Form the batter into one or more of the shapes suggested below.

Tulipes. For each biscuit, drop a heaped tablespoon of batter on to the prepared baking sheet and spread as directed in the technique (*left*). Make no more than three biscuits at a time. Bake them until the edges are delicately browned — about 5 minutes. Shape the biscuits as shown in the technique. (If they become too stiff to shape, return briefly to the oven to soften — about 30 seconds — before continuing.) Repeat the process for the remaining batter. Fill the *tulipes* with ice cream, sorbet or berries just before serving.

Oak leaves. Use an oak-leaf stencil as shown (*left*) to shape the biscuits. Such a stencil can be purchased at kitchen shops, or made by tracing an oak leaf on cardboard and cutting out the shape. For the veins, put 1 tablespoon of the batter into a small bowl and sift in the cocoa, then mix the cocoa thoroughly into the batter with a spoon. Use the tip of a small spoon or knife to paint each biscuit with veins as directed. Bake the leaves until they are delicately browned at the edges — about 5 minutes.

Remove the baking sheet and set it on the stove top so it stays warm. Loosen an oak leaf with a metal spatula; working quickly, curl the leaf by bending it over a counter edge. (If the biscuits become too stiff to shape, return them briefly to the oven to soften — about 30 seconds — before continuing.) Shape, bake and curl the remaining biscuits in the same way.

Cigarettes. For each cigarette, drop a scant tablespoon of the batter on to a prepared baking sheet and spread it as shown (*left*). Bake until the edges are delicately browned — about 5 minutes. Shape the cigarettes as directed in the technique. (If the biscuits become too stiff, return them briefly to the oven to soften — about 30 seconds — before continuing.)

Per tulipe:
Calories **70**
Protein **1g**
Cholesterol **10mg**
Total fat **4g**
Saturated fat **2g**
Sodium **8mg**

Per leaf:
Calories **50**
Protein **1g**
Cholesterol **8mg**
Total fat **3g**
Saturated fat **2g**
Sodium **6mg**

Per cigarette:
Calories **45**
Protein **1g**
Cholesterol **7mg**
Total fat **3g**
Saturated fat **2g**
Sodium **6mg**

EDITOR'S NOTE: *Store the biscuits in an airtight container.*

3

Light and Creamy Favourites

Not the least of a dessert's appeal is its texture. The fluffier and creamier the dessert, the more seductive it is likely to be. But all too often people regard such a dessert as an indulgence, equating its creaminess with richness. In this section, you will find recipes for light and creamy desserts that are delightfully low in calories, yet deliver their full amount of satisfaction — mousses, a layered Bavarian, fruit-filled soufflés, even some ethereal cheesecakes. Complementing them are several sturdier desserts: puddings that invoke childhood memories, but with provocative surprises, such as the rice pudding with raspberry sauce on page 89, or the buttermilk sauce that accompanies the Indian pudding on page 103.

Many of these desserts share an ingredient that entails no fat, no calories and no cost — air. Its presence, in large quantities, may define the very character of a dessert. A soufflé — French for "blown" or "whispered" — is basically a structure of egg whites beaten stiff to entrap a maximum of air. During baking, the air heats and expands to push the dessert mixture to new heights.

Beaten egg whites are folded into many other desserts to lighten them, occasionally along with dissolved gelatine for firmness or a little whipped cream for a velvet texture. Or, more elaborately, the whites may be used as the base for an Italian meringue, itself the base of several desserts featured here. In preparing Italian meringue, the whites and hot sugar syrup are beaten simultaneously to make a mixture that is more stable than a meringue made with uncooked sugar. Do not let the sugar syrup hit the whisk or beaters as you add it to the whites; if it does, it may splatter on to the sides of the bowl and stick there — or, worse, it may burn the cook. Where the recipes call for whipping cream, make sure that the cream is cold, and that the bowl and beaters are too.

Many of the recipes in this section involve the use of a mould. Unmoulding the dessert can be as easy as covering the top of the mould with an inverted plate, then turning the mould over and giving it a gentle shake. If the dessert is unyielding, try briefly dipping the bottom of the mould into warm water, or wrap the mould in a damp, hot towel. Failing this, run the tip of a knife round the edge of the mould to break the vacuum that may be keeping the dessert from sliding free.

Baked Chocolate Custards

Serves 8
Working time: about 30 minutes
Total time: about 2 hours

Calories **110**
Protein **4g**
Cholesterol **75mg**
Total fat **3g**
Saturated fat **1g**
Sodium **70mg**

2	eggs	2
100 g	caster sugar	3½ oz
2 tbsp	unsweetened cocoa powder	2 tbsp
1/16 tsp	salt	1/16 tsp
½ litre	semi-skimmed milk	16 fl oz
45 g	fresh raspberries (optional)	1½ oz

Preheat the oven to 170°C (325°F or Mark 3). Whisk together the eggs, sugar, cocoa powder and salt in a heatproof bowl. Heat the milk in a small saucepan just until it comes to the boil. Whisking continuously, pour the hot milk into the bowl. Thoroughly mix in the milk, then pour the mixture into the saucepan.

Cook the mixture over low heat, stirring constantly with a wooden spoon, until it has thickened enough to lightly coat the back of the spoon. Strain the mixture into eight individual ovenproof custard cups or ramekins. Set the custard cups in a roasting pan or casserole with sides at least 1 cm (½ inch) higher than the cups. Pour enough boiling water into the pan to come half way up the sides of the cups. Cover the pan with a baking sheet or a piece of aluminium foil, then put it in the oven, and bake the custards until the centre of one barely quivers when the cup is shaken — 20 to 30 minutes.

Remove the pan from the oven and uncover it. Leave the custard cups in the water until they cool to room temperature, then refrigerate them for at least 30 minutes. If you like, arrange several fresh raspberries on each custard before serving them.

Amaretto Custards with Plum Sauce

Serves 6
Working time: about 30 minutes
Total time: about 1 hour and 30 minutes

Calories **250**	25 g	almonds, sliced	¾ oz
Protein **8g**	1¼ tsp	ground cinnamon	1¼ tsp
Cholesterol **100mg**	5 tbsp	caster sugar	5 tbsp
Total fat **7g**	2	eggs, plus 2 egg whites	2
Saturated fat **2g**	4 tbsp	amaretto liqueur	4 tbsp
Sodium **95mg**	90 g	honey	3 oz
	55 cl	semi-skimmed milk	18 fl oz
	4	ripe red plums, quartered and stoned	4
	2 tsp	fresh lemon juice	2 tsp

Preheat the oven to 170°C (325°F or Mark 3). Spread the almonds in a small baking tin and toast them in the oven as it preheats until they are golden — about 25 minutes.

Lightly butter six 12.5 cl (4 fl oz) ramekins, or other individual ovenproof moulds. In a small dish, mix ¾ teaspoon of the cinnamon with 2 tablespoons of the sugar. Put about 1 teaspoon of the cinnamon-and-sugar mixture into each ramekin or mould, then tilt it in all directions to coat its buttered sides and bottom. Put the ramekins into a large, ovenproof baking dish and refrigerate them.

In a large bowl, whisk together the eggs, egg whites, amaretto, honey and the remaining ½ teaspoon of cinnamon. Whisk in the milk, then pour the mixture into the chilled ramekins, filling each to within 5 mm (¼ inch) of the top.

Place the baking dish with the filled ramekins in the preheated oven. Pour enough hot tap water into the baking dish to come two thirds of the way up the sides of the ramekins. Bake the custards until a thin-bladed knife inserted in the centre of one comes out clean — about 30 minutes. Remove the ramekins from their water bath and let them stand for half an hour.

While the custards cool, prepare the plum sauce. Combine the plums, the remaining 3 tablespoons of sugar and the lemon juice in a food processor or a blender. Process the plums to a smooth purée, then pass the purée through a fine sieve into a bowl to remove the skins. Refrigerate the sauce until it is chilled — about half an hour.

To unmould the cooled custards, run a small, sharp knife round the inside of each ramekin. Invert a serving plate over the top and turn both over together. Lift away the ramekin; the custard should slip out easily. If it does not, rock the ramekin from side to side to loosen it. Ladle some of the plum sauce round each custard; sprinkle the toasted almonds over the top.

Lemon-Buttermilk Custards with Candied Lemon Slices

Serves 8
Working time: about 20 minutes
Total time: about 2 hours and 40 minutes
(includes chilling)

Calories **185**
Protein **5g**
Cholesterol **70mg**
Total fat **2g**
Saturated fat **1g**
Sodium **115mg**

2	eggs	2
200 g	caster sugar	7 oz
45 g	plain flour	1½ oz
2 tsp	pure lemon extract	2 tsp
¾ litre	buttermilk	1¼ pints
3	lemons, thinly sliced, for garnish	3
60 g	raspberries for garnish	2 oz

Preheat the oven to 150°C (300°F or Mark 2).

To prepare the custard, first whisk the eggs in a bowl, then whisk in 135 g (4½ oz) of the sugar and the flour; when the custard is smooth, stir in the lemon extract and buttermilk. Pour the custard into eight 12.5 cl (4 fl oz) ramekins and set them on a baking sheet. Bake the custards until they are puffed up and set, and a knife inserted at the edge comes out clean — 15 to 20 minutes. Let the custards cool slightly, then refrigerate them until they are well chilled — about 2 hours.

To make the candied lemon slices, lightly oil a baking sheet and set it aside. Combine the remaining sugar with 4 tablespoons of water in a small, heavy-bottomed saucepan. Bring the mixture to the boil, then reduce the heat to low and cook, stirring occasionally, until the sugar has dissolved and the syrup is clear — about 1½ minutes. Add the lemon slices to the pan; immediately turn the slices over, coating them well, and cook them for about 30 seconds. Transfer the slices to the oiled baking sheet.

To serve, run a small knife round the inside of each ramekin and invert the custards on to serving plates. Garnish each plate with a few candied lemon slices and a sprinkling of fresh raspberries.

Rice Pudding with Raspberry Sauce

THIS VARIATION ON AN OLD DESSERT OWES ITS VELVETY
TEXTURE TO THE INCLUSION OF PASTRY CREAM.

Serves 8
Working time: about 50 minutes
Total time: about 3 hours

Calories **225**
Protein **7g**
Cholesterol **45mg**
Total fat **3g**
Saturated fat **2g**
Sodium **140mg**

1 litre	semi-skimmed milk	1¾ pints
90 g	long-grain rice	3 oz
125 g	sugar	4 oz
¼ tsp	salt	¼ tsp
1	egg yolk	1
3 tbsp	plain flour	3 tbsp
½ tsp	grated nutmeg	½ tsp
1 tsp	pure vanilla extract	1 tsp
¼ tsp	almond extract	¼ tsp
45 g	sultanas	1½ oz
250 g	fresh or frozen whole raspberries, thawed	8 oz
	fresh mint leaves (optional)	

Bring ¾ litre (1¼ pints) of the milk to the boil in a
heavy-bottomed saucepan over medium heat. Reduce
the heat to low and add the rice, 50 g (1½ oz) of the
sugar and the salt. Cook the mixture, stirring frequently, for 50 minutes.

To prepare the pastry cream, whisk together the egg
yolk and 4 tablespoons of the remaining milk. Whisk in
the flour and 50 g (1½ oz) of the remaining sugar;
then blend in the remaining milk. Bring the mixture to
the boil over medium heat, stirring constantly, then
cook it, still stirring vigorously, for 2 minutes more.
Remove the pan from the heat and stir in the nutmeg,
and vanilla and almond extracts.

When the rice has finished cooking, stir in the
sultanas, then fold in the pastry cream. Transfer the
pudding to a clean bowl. To prevent a skin from
forming on its surface, press a sheet of plastic film
directly on to the pudding. Refrigerate the pudding
until it is cold — about 2 hours.

To prepare the sauce, purée the raspberries and the remaining 25 g (1 oz) sugar in a blender or food processor.
Rub the purée through a fine sieve with a plastic spatula
or the back of a wooden spoon; discard the seeds.

To serve, divide the sauce among eight serving
dishes. Top the sauce with individual scoops of pudding; if you like, sprinkle the scoops with some additional nutmeg and garnish each with a sprig of mint.

Cheese Valentine
with Blackberries

THIS DESSERT, MADE IN A *COEUR À FROMAGE* MOULD, CONTAINS
GOAT CHEESE AND GOES PARTICULARLY WELL WITH TART, FRESH FRUIT.

Serves 10
Working time: about 20 minutes
Total time: about 6 hours (includes chilling)

750 g	low-fat cottage cheese	1½ lb
175 g	mild, creamy goat cheese	6 oz
4 tbsp	caster sugar	4 tbsp
600 g	blackberries or strawberries	1¼ lb

Purée the cottage cheese in a food processor or a blender until it is completely smooth. With the motor running, blend in the goat cheese a tablespoon at a time. Stop once or twice during the process to scrape down the sides. Add the sugar and blend it in.

Cut a single thickness of muslin large enough to encase the cheese mixture as it drains. Wet the muslin in cold water, then wring it out. Line a large *coeur à fromage* mould, sieve or colander with the muslin, pressing it in place and smoothing it out with your fingers so that the surface of the finished cheese will be uniformly even.

Spoon the cheese mixture into the lined container. Smooth the top of the cheese mixture and fold the edges of the muslin over it. If you are using a sieve or colander, place it over a deep bowl; if you are using a *coeur à fromage* mould, put it on a plate. Refrigerate the assembly until the whey has thoroughly drained from the cheese — about 6 hours.

To unmould the drained cheese, open the muslin and invert a serving plate over the mould or sieve. Turn both mould and plate over together, then lift away the mould and the muslin.

Serve the valentine chilled. Ring the plate with some of the berries; present the rest in a separate dish.

Maple Mousse with Glazed Apple Nuggets

Serves 6
Working time: about 1 hour
Total time: about 1 hour and 45 minutes

15 g	unsalted butter	½ oz
2	tart green apples, peeled, cored and cut into 1 cm (½ inch) cubes	2
1 tsp	fresh lemon juice	1 tsp
175 g	maple syrup	6 oz
6 tbsp	double cream	6 tbsp
½ tsp	pure vanilla extract	½ tsp
3	egg whites, at room temperature	3
5 tbsp	light brown sugar	5 tbsp

Melt the butter in a large, heavy frying pan set over medium-high heat. When the butter is hot, add the apple cubes and lemon juice; sauté the cubes, turning them frequently, until they are light brown — about 10 minutes. Dribble 1 tablespoon of the maple syrup over the apple cubes and sauté them for 1 minute more. Transfer the glazed apple cubes to a plate and refrigerate them.

In a small bowl, whip the cream until it holds stiff peaks, stir in the vanilla extract, then refrigerate the cream. Put the egg whites into a deep bowl and set them aside.

To prepare the maple flavouring for the mousse, combine half of the remaining maple syrup and the sugar in a small, heavy-bottomed saucepan. Bring the mixture to the boil and cook it to the soft-ball stage over medium heat *(page 95)*. Begin testing after 4 minutes: with a small spoon, drop a bit of the syrup into a bowl filled with iced water. When the mixture can be rolled into a ball, start beating the egg whites with an electric mixer on medium-high speed. Pour the hot syrup into the whites in a thin, steady stream, beating as you pour. Continue to beat the whites until the meringue has cooled to room temperature — about 7 minutes. Gently fold the whipped cream and the chilled apple pieces into the meringue. (Do not overfold.) Immediately spoon the mousse into six individual dishes and refrigerate them for at least 45 minutes.

To prepare the maple sugar, bring the remaining syrup to the boil in a small, heavy-bottomed saucepan. Reduce the heat to medium and cook the syrup, stirring frequently, until the mixture crystallizes — about 15 minutes. Remove the saucepan from the heat and allow the mixture to cool for 10 minutes, stirring occasionally. Scrape the crystallized sugar out of the pan on to a clean work surface. Using a rolling pin or the bottom of a heavy pan, crush the sugar until it is finely crumbled.

Just before serving, sprinkle some of the maple sugar on to each portion of mousse.

Banana Crème Caramel

Serves 8
Working time: about 45 minutes
Total time: about 3 hours and 15 minutes

Calories **160**
Protein **3g**
Cholesterol **70mg**
Total fat **2g**
Saturated fat **1g**
Sodium **35mg**

165 g	sugar	5½ oz
4 tsp	fresh lemon juice	4 tsp
¼ litre	semi-skimmed milk	8 fl oz
2	eggs	2
1 tbsp	dark rum	1 tbsp
1 tsp	pure vanilla extract	1 tsp
¼ tsp	ground cardamom or cinnamon	¼ tsp
¼ litre	puréed banana (from 2 to 3 bananas)	8 fl oz
2	bananas, peeled and diagonally sliced	2

Preheat the oven to 170°C (325°F or Mark 3).

Begin by caramelizing a 1 litre (2 pint) soufflé dish or a 15 cm (6 inch) diameter cake tin. In a small heavy-bottomed saucepan, combine 100 g (3½ oz) of the sugar, 1 teaspoon of the lemon juice and 3 tablespoons of water. Cook the mixture over medium-high heat until the syrup caramelizes — it will have a rich brown hue. Immediately remove the saucepan from the heat. Working quickly, pour the caramel into the soufflé dish or cake tin. Using oven gloves to protect your hands, tilt the dish in all directions to coat the bottom and about 2.5 cm (1 inch) of the adjacent sides. Continue tilting the dish until the caramel has hardened, then set the dish aside.

To prepare the custard, put the milk into a heavy-bottomed saucepan over medium heat. As soon as the milk reaches the boil, remove the pan from the heat and set it aside. In a bowl, whisk together the eggs and the remaining sugar, then stir in the rum, vanilla extract, cardamom or cinnamon, puréed banana, and the remaining 3 teaspoons of lemon juice. Stirring constantly to avoid curdling the eggs, pour the hot milk into the banana mixture. Transfer the custard to the caramelized dish.

Set the custard dish in a small roasting pan and pour enough hot tap water into the pan to come 2.5 cm (1 inch) up the sides of the custard dish. Bake the custard until a knife inserted in the centre comes out clean — 20 to 30 minutes. (Take care not to insert the knife so deep that it pierces the caramel coating.) Remove the custard from the hot-water bath and let it cool to room temperature. Put the custard into the refrigerator until it is chilled — about 2 hours.

To unmould, invert a serving plate over the top of the dish, then turn both over together. The dish should lift away easily; if not, turn the dish right side up again and run a small, sharp knife round the top of the custard to loosen it. Garnish with a ring of banana slices. Cut the custard into wedges and spoon some of the caramel sauce over each one before serving.

Raspberry Mousse

Serves 8
Working time: about 20 minutes
Total time: about 1 hour

2½ tsp	powdered gelatine	2½ tsp
100 g	sugar	3½ oz
400 g	fresh or frozen whole raspberries, thawed	14 oz
¼ litre	plain low-fat yogurt	8 fl oz
12.5 cl	double cream	4 fl oz
2	egg whites	2

Calories **150**
Protein **4g**
Cholesterol **25mg**
Total fat **6g**
Saturated fat **4g**
Sodium **40mg**

Sprinkle the gelatine on to 4 tablespoons of water and let the gelatine soften while you prepare the raspberries. Set 24 berries aside to use as garnish. Pour 4 tablespoons of water into a saucepan; stir in the sugar and the remaining raspberries. Over medium heat, simmer the mixture for 4 minutes. Add the softened gelatine and stir until it dissolves — about 30 seconds.

Transfer the raspberry mixture to a blender or a food processor and purée it. Strain the purée through a fine sieve into a bowl. Refrigerate the purée until it is cool, then stir in the yogurt.

Whip the cream until it forms stiff peaks. Fold the whipped cream into the raspberry mixture.

Beat the egg whites in a bowl until stiff peaks form when the beater is lifted from the bowl. Fold the egg whites into the raspberry mixture *(page 103)*.

Fill each of eight wine glasses with the raspberry mousse. Chill the mousse for at least 30 minutes; just before serving, garnish each mousse with three of the reserved raspberries.

Chilled Lemon Mousse with Blueberries

Serves 8
Working time: about 35 minutes
Total time: about 1 hour and 30 minutes

2	lemons	2
1	egg, plus 1 egg white	1
225 g	caster sugar	7½ oz
60 g	unsalted butter, melted	2 oz
500 g	fresh blueberries, picked over and rinsed	1 lb
4	egg whites	4
⅛ tsp	cream of tartar	⅛ tsp

Calories **215**
Protein **3g**
Cholesterol **50mg**
Total fat **7g**
Saturated fat **4g**
Sodium **45mg**

Grate the rind of the lemons and put it in the top of a double boiler. Squeeze the juice from the lemons and add it to the rind. Whisk the egg, egg white and 200 g (7 oz) of the sugar into the lemon mixture, and set it over simmering water. Cook the mixture, stirring continuously, until it thickens — 12 to 15 minutes. (Do not overcook the mixture or it will curdle.)

Remove the double boiler from the heat and mix in the butter. Set the top of the double boiler in a larger bowl filled with ice and let the mixture cool, whisking it occasionally.

To prepare the meringue, put the egg whites and the cream of tartar into a bowl, and beat them until soft peaks form. Add a little of the remaining sugar and continue beating the egg whites, gradually adding the rest of the sugar, until stiff peaks have formed and the meringue is glossy.

Stir a few heaped spoonfuls of the meringue into the cooled lemon mixture to lighten it *(page 103)*. Fold in the remaining meringue and all but 90 g (3 oz) of the blueberries. Spoon the lemon mousse into parfait glasses and chill for at least 1 hour before serving. Garnish each serving with a few of the reserved blueberries.

Layered Bavarian

Serves 8
Working time: about 1 hour
Total time: about 4 hours and 30 minutes
(includes chilling)

500 g	ripe apricots or nectarines	1 lb
1 tbsp	fresh lemon juice	1 tbsp
3 tbsp	powdered gelatine	3 tbsp
¾ litre	plain low-fat yogurt	1¼ pints
2 tbsp	honey	2 tbsp
1 tsp	pure vanilla extract	1 tsp
300 g	blackberries, picked over and stemmed	10 oz
1 tbsp	fresh lime juice	1 tbsp
3	egg whites	3
100 g	sugar	3½ oz
3	apricots, or 2 nectarines, thinly sliced, for garnish (optional)	3

Calories **185**
Protein **10g**
Cholesterol **5mg**
Total fat **2g**
Saturated fat **1g**
Sodium **85mg**

Bring 4 litres (7 pints) of water to the boil in a large pan. Add the apricots or nectarines and blanch them until their skins loosen — 30 seconds to 1 minute. Remove the apricots or nectarines from the water; when they are cool enough to handle, peel them and cut them in half, discarding the stones and skins. Purée the halves with the lemon juice in a food processor or a blender.

Pour 2 tablespoons of water into a small saucepan. Sprinkle in 1 tablespoon of the gelatine. Heat the mixture over low heat, stirring continuously until the gelatine has dissolved. Blend the gelatine mixture and 12.5 cl (4 fl oz) of the yogurt into the fruit purée. Set the mixture aside.

In a bowl, combine ½ litre (16 fl oz) of the remaining yogurt with the honey and vanilla. Pour 2 tablespoons of water into a small saucepan and sprinkle in 1 tablespoon of the remaining gelatine. Heat the mixture over low heat to dissolve the gelatine, then whisk it into the yogurt-honey mixture. Set this mixture aside.

Heat the blackberries and lime juice in a small, non-reactive saucepan over medium heat until the berries render their juice — about 5 minutes. Purée the berries and juice in a food processor or a blender, then strain the purée through a fine sieve.

Pour 2 tablespoons of water into a small saucepan; sprinkle in the remaining tablespoon of gelatine, and heat the mixture over low heat until the gelatine dissolves. Blend this gelatine mixture and the remaining yogurt into the blackberry purée. Set the blackberry mixture aside.

Pour the egg whites into a deep bowl. Set up an electric mixer; you will need to start beating the egg whites as soon as the syrup is ready.

To prepare Italian meringue *(below)*, heat the sugar with 4 tablespoons of water in a small saucepan over medium-high heat. Boil the mixture until the bubbles rise to the surface in a random pattern, indicating that the water has nearly evaporated and the sugar itself is beginning to cook.

With a small spoon, drop a little of the syrup into a bowl of iced water. If the syrup dissolves instantly, continue cooking it. When the syrup dropped into the water can be rolled between your fingers into a supple ball, begin beating the egg whites on high speed. Pour the syrup down the side of the bowl in a thin, steady stream. When all the syrup has been incorporated, decrease the speed to medium; continue beating the ▶

Making Italian Meringue

1 *TESTING THE SYRUP. In a heavy-bottomed pan, cook the sugar syrup until the surface bubbles continuously. To test for the "soft-ball" stage, drop a spoonful into iced water. Gather it up in a ball with your fingers and remove from the water. It should hold together yet feel pliable and sticky. The soft-ball stage is reached between 112° and 116°C (234° and 240°F) on a sugar thermometer.*

2 *POURING IN THE SYRUP. As soon as the sugar has reached the soft-ball stage, start beating the egg whites at high speed in a bowl. Pour the hot syrup into the bowl in a slow, steady stream, avoiding the beater heads. After the syrup has been added, reduce the mixer speed to medium.*

3 *TESTING THE MERINGUE. Keep beating the mixture on medium until it cools to room temperature: test the temperature by feeling the sides of the bowl with your hand. Then beat the mixture at high speed for 1 minute to stiffen it. The mixture will have frothed into a smooth, thick meringue and should hold stiff, glossy peaks.*

egg whites until they are glossy, have formed stiff peaks and have cooled to room temperature — at least 5 minutes. Increase the speed to high and beat the meringue for 1 minute more.

Fold one third of the meringue into each of the prepared mixtures. Do not refrigerate any of the mixtures.

Rinse a 2 litre (3½ pint) mould under cold running water. Shake it dry; to facilitate unmoulding the finished dessert, do not wipe it dry. Pour the apricot or nectarine mixture into the mould and refrigerate it for 45 minutes. Next, pour in the vanilla mixture and refrigerate the mould for 45 minutes more. Finally, pour the

blackberry mixture into the mould, forming the third layer, and chill in the refrigerator for at least 2 hours.

Unmould the Bavarian as close to serving time as possible: dip the bottom of the mould into hot water for 15 seconds, then run the tip of a knife round the inside edge of the mould to break the air lock. Invert a chilled platter on top, and turn both platter and mould over together. If the Bavarian does not come free, wrap the mould in a towel that has been soaked with hot water and wrung out. After 15 seconds, remove the towel and lift away the mould. If you like, garnish the Bavarian with apricot or nectarine slices.

Orange and Buttermilk Parfaits

Serves 8
Working time: about 40 minutes
Total time: about 1 hour and 10 minutes

Calories **145**
Protein **5g**
Cholesterol **70mg**
Total fat **2g**
Saturated fat **1g**
Sodium **75mg**

35 cl	buttermilk	12 fl oz
½ tbsp	powdered gelatine	½ tbsp
150 g	sugar	5 oz
2	eggs, separated, plus 1 egg white	2
4 tbsp	frozen orange juice concentrate, thawed	4 tbsp
2	oranges, for garnish	2

Put ¼ litre (8 fl oz) of the buttermilk, the gelatine, 4 tablespoons of the sugar and the egg yolks into a

small, heavy-bottomed saucepan over low heat. Cook the mixture, stirring constantly with a wooden spoon, until it is thick enough to coat the back of the spoon — 6 to 8 minutes. (Do not let the mixture come to the boil or it will curdle.) Divide the mixture between two bowls. Whisk the remaining buttermilk into one of the bowls; whisk the orange juice concentrate into the other. Set both bowls aside at room temperature.

Make Italian meringue *(page 95)*. First, pour the egg whites into a deep bowl. Then set up an electric mixer; you will need to start beating the egg whites as soon as the syrup is ready.

Heat the remaining sugar with 4 tablespoons of water in a small, heavy-bottomed saucepan over medium-high heat. Boil the mixture until the bubbles rise to the surface in a random pattern, indicating that the water has nearly evaporated and the sugar itself is beginning to cook. With a small spoon, drop a little of the syrup into a bowl filled with iced water. If the syrup dissolves immediately, continue cooking. When the syrup dropped into the water can be rolled between your fingers into a supple ball, start the mixer.

Begin beating the egg whites at high speed. Pour the syrup into the bowl in a very thin, steady stream. When all the syrup has been incorporated, decrease the speed to medium; continue beating until the egg whites are glossy, have formed stiff peaks and have cooled to room temperature. Increase the speed to high and beat the meringue for 1 minute more.

Mix a few heaped spoonfuls of the meringue into each of the buttermilk mixtures to lighten them. Fold half of the remaining meringue into each mixture.

Spoon the mixture containing the extra buttermilk into eight glasses and top it with the orange mixture. Refrigerate the parfaits for at least 30 minutes.

For the garnish, segment the two oranges as demonstrated on page 14. Just before serving, garnish each portion with orange segments.

Raspberry Soufflés

Serves 6
Working time: about 30 minutes
Total time: about 1 hour and 10 minutes

125 g	caster sugar	4 oz
250 g	fresh or frozen whole raspberries, thawed	8 oz
2	egg whites	2
6 tbsp	icing sugar	6 tbsp

Calories **45**
Protein **0g**
Cholesterol **0mg**
Total fat **0g**
Saturated fat **0g**
Sodium **6mg**

Lightly butter six 12.5 cl (4 fl oz) ramekins. Divide 2 tablespoons of the sugar evenly among the ramekins, then tilt and rotate the ramekins to coat them thoroughly with the sugar. Set the ramekins on a baking sheet and refrigerate them.

Purée the raspberries in a food processor or a blender. Strain the purée through a fine sieve and set it aside. Preheat the oven to 200°C (400°F or Mark 6).

Pour the egg whites into a deep bowl. Set up an electric mixer; you will need to start beating the egg whites as soon as the syrup is ready.

To prepare Italian meringue (page 95), heat the remaining sugar with 4 tablespoons of water in a small saucepan over medium-high heat. Boil the mixture until the bubbles rise to the surface in a random pattern, indicating that the water has nearly evaporated and the sugar itself is beginning to cook.

With a small spoon, drop a little of the syrup into a bowl of iced water. If the syrup dissolves immediately, continue cooking. When the syrup dropped into the water can be rolled between your fingers into a supple ball, begin beating the egg whites on high speed. Pour the syrup down the side of the bowl in a very thin, steady stream. When all the syrup has been incorporated, decrease the speed to medium; continue beating the egg whites until they are glossy, have formed stiff peaks and have cooled to room temperature — 5 to 10 minutes. Increase the speed to high and beat the meringue for 1 minute more.

Stir about one third of the meringue into the raspberry purée to lighten it, then fold in the remaining meringue. Divide the soufflé mixture among the prepared ramekins, slightly overfilling each one. Level their tops with a spatula, then run the tip of your thumb round the inside edge of each ramekin; the resulting circular depression will keep the edges of the soufflés from burning as the depressions puff up in the oven. Sift 1 tablespoon of the icing sugar over the top of each soufflé; bake the soufflés until they have risen and are set — about 10 minutes. Serve the soufflés immediately.

EDITOR'S NOTE: If it is inconvenient to serve the finished soufflés at once, keep them from collapsing by leaving them in the oven with the heat turned off and the door open.

Mile-High Pie with Two Sauces

Serves 12
Working time: about 1 hour
Total time: about 2 hours

Calories **240**
Protein **6g**
Cholesterol **70mg**
Total fat **3g**
Saturated fat **1g**
Sodium **85mg**

1 tbsp	safflower oil	1 tbsp
315 g	caster sugar	10½ oz
12	egg whites	12
1 tbsp	pure vanilla extract	1 tbsp
¼ tsp	cream of tartar	¼ tsp
Vanilla-yogurt sauce		
30 cl	semi-skimmed milk	½ pint
1	vanilla pod	1
3	egg yolks	3
2 tbsp	caster sugar	2 tbsp
¼ litre	plain low-fat yogurt	8 fl oz
Cranberry sauce		
200 g	fresh or frozen cranberries, picked over	7 oz
100 g	caster sugar	3½ oz
12.5 cl	ruby port	4 fl oz
6 tbsp	plain low-fat yogurt	6 tbsp

Brush the inside of a 23 cm (9 inch) springform tin with the oil. Sprinkle in 15 g (½ oz) of the sugar; shake and tilt the pan to coat it evenly with the sugar. Preheat the oven to 150°C (300°F or Mark 2).

To prepare the meringue, put the egg whites, vanilla extract and cream of tartar into a bowl. Begin beating the whites at low speed, gradually increasing the speed to medium as the whites turn opaque. Add the remaining 300 g (10 oz) of sugar a tablespoon at a time, increasing the beater speed all the while. When all the sugar has been incorporated, continue beating the whites on high speed until they are glossy and form stiff peaks when the beater is lifted from the bowl.

Transfer the meringue to the springform tin. Smooth the top of the meringue with a long spatula or the dull side of a knife. Bake the pie until it has risen and is lightly browned — about 40 minutes. It will be moist throughout. Remove the pie from the oven and let it cool to room temperature in the tin.

While the pie is baking and cooling, make the sauces. To make the vanilla-yogurt sauce, heat the milk, vanilla pod, egg yolks and sugar in a small, heavy-bottomed, non-reactive saucepan set over low heat. Cook the mixture, stirring constantly with a wooden spoon, until it is thick enough to coat the back of the spoon. Strain the sauce into a bowl and set it aside; when it has cooled to room temperature, whisk in the yogurt.

To make the cranberry sauce, cook the cranberries, sugar and 12.5 cl (4 fl oz) of water in a small saucepan over medium-high heat. Cook the cranberries until they burst — 6 to 8 minutes. Continue cooking the berries until they are quite soft — about 5 minutes.

Press the cooked berries through a sieve into a bowl and set them aside. When they have cooled to room temperature, whisk in the port and the yogurt.

Just before serving the pie, remove the sides of the tin. With a wet knife, cut the pie into wedges; present them with the vanilla-yogurt sauce and the cranberry sauce poured round them. If you like, swirl the two sauces together as shown below.

Two Methods for Swirling Sauces

A Carousel of Hearts

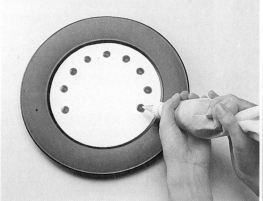

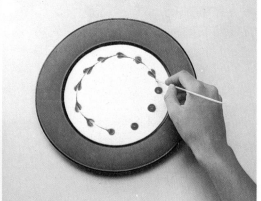

1 PIPING THE SAUCE. Shortly before serving the dessert, pour sauce into the centre of a plate. Tip and swirl the plate to cover the bottom evenly. Pour sauce of a contrasting colour into a piping bag with a very small plain nozzle, as here, or into a plastic squeeze bottle. Pipe a ring of dots on to the first sauce (above).

2 CONNECTING THE DOTS. With one steady motion, draw the blunt end of a wooden skewer or toothpick from the centre of one dot through the centre of the next dot in the ring. Continue connecting the dots, without lifting the skewer, until you have formed a wreath of linked hearts. Set the dessert in the middle.

A Rippled Kaleidoscope

1 CREATING A SPIRAL. Fill a plate with sauce as in Step 1 above. Pour a sauce of contrasting colour into a plastic squeeze bottle, as here, or into a piping bag with a very small plain nozzle. Practice an even flow by squeezing some of the sauce on to a paper towel in a smooth line. Starting at the centre of the plate, squeeze out the sauce in a continuous spiral.

2 RIPPLING THE SPIRAL. Draw the blunt end of a wooden skewer or toothpick from the centre of the spiral to its rim. Lift the skewer from the surface of the sauce, reinsert it about 2.5 cm (1 inch) farther along the rim, and draw the skewer from the rim to the centre. Repeat the process to divide the spiral into about a dozen rippled wedges of equal size. Set the dessert in the middle of the design.

Put the egg whites into a deep bowl. Set up an electric mixer; you will need to start beating the egg whites as soon as the syrup is ready.

To prepare Italian meringue *(page 95),* heat the remaining sugar with 2 tablespoons of water in a small saucepan over medium-high heat. Boil the mixture until the bubbles rise to the surface in a random pattern, indicating that the water has nearly evaporated and the sugar is beginning to cook.

With a small spoon, drop a little of the syrup into a bowl filled with iced water. If the syrup dissolves immediately, continue cooking the syrup. When the syrup dropped into the water can be rolled between your fingers into a supple ball, begin beating the egg whites on high speed. Pour the syrup down the side of the bowl in a thin, steady stream. When all the syrup has been incorporated, decrease the speed to medium continue beating until the egg whites are glossy, have formed stiff peaks and have cooled to room temperature — about 10 minutes. Increase the speed to high and beat the meringue for 1 minute more.

Line a 20 cm (8 inch) cake tin with plastic film. Drain the sultanas and raisins and scatter them in the bottom of the tin. Mix about one third of the meringue into the cheese mixture to lighten it. Gently fold in the rest of the meringue, then pour the cheesecake mixture into the lined tin. Chill the cheesecake for 4 hours.

To turn out the cheesecake, invert a serving plate on top of the tin then turn both over together. Lift away the tin, peel off the plastic film, and slice the cheesecake for serving.

Raisin Cheesecake

Serves 12
Working time: about 1 hour
Total time: about 5 hours (includes chilling)

Calories **120**
Protein **7g**
Cholesterol **11mg**
Total fat **3g**
Saturated fat **2g**
Sodium **150mg**

45 g	sultanas	1½ oz
45 g	raisins	1½ oz
¼ litre	plain low-fat yogurt	8 fl oz
90 g	low-fat creamy soft cheese	3 oz
300 g	low-fat cottage cheese	10 oz
1 tsp	pure vanilla extract	1 tsp
100 g	caster sugar	3½ oz
12.5 cl	semi-skimmed milk	4 fl oz
1 tbsp	powdered gelatine	1 tbsp
3	egg whites, at room temperature	3

Put the sultanas and raisins in a small bowl and pour ¼ litre (8 fl oz) of hot water over them. Set the bowl aside.

Purée the yogurt, soft cheese, cottage cheese, vanilla extract and half the sugar in a food processor or a blender. Scrape the cheese mixture into a large bowl.

Pour the milk into a small saucepan. Sprinkle the gelatine over the milk and let it stand until the gelatine softens — about 5 minutes. Heat the milk over medium heat, stirring until the gelatine is dissolved. Stir the milk into the cheese mixture and set it aside.

Home-Made Yogurt

Makes 1 litre (1¾ pints)
Working time: about 20 minutes
Total time: about 3 hours and 20 minutes

Per ¼ litre (8 fl oz)
Calories **230**
Protein **13g**
Cholesterol **20mg**
Total fat **5g**
Saturated fat **3g**
Sodium **225mg**

90 g	dried skimmed milk	3
1 litre	semi-skimmed milk	1¾ pir
3 tbsp	live plain low-fat yogurt	3 tb

Combine the dried milk and the liquid milk, stirring until the dried milk is completely dissolved. Gently heat the milk until it registers between 43° and 47°C (110 and 115°F) on a sugar thermometer, then remove from the heat. Stir a little of the warm milk into the yogurt to temper it, then add the yogurt to the remaining warm milk. Gently stir the mixture until it smooth; pour it into two clean ½ litre (16 fl oz) jars Cover the jars tightly and put them in a warm place — on top of your refrigerator for example; 32°C (90°F) ideal — for 3 to 5 hours.

To test the yogurt for doneness, tilt one of the jar the liquid whey should have separated from the sol curd. Press the curd with your finger — it should be firm. If the yogurt is still semi-liquid, return the jar the warm place until the curd sets. Pour off the whe then cover the jars and store them in the refrigerator

Blackberry Timbales with Almond Cream

Serves 8
Working time: about 45 minutes
Total time: about 2 hours and 45 minutes
(includes chilling)

Calories **280**
Protein **9g**
Cholesterol **30mg**
Total fat **8g**
Saturated fat **5g**
Sodium **170mg**

5 tsp	powdered gelatine	5 tsp
300 g	blackberries	10 oz
135 g	caster sugar	4½ oz
¼ tsp	salt	¼ tsp
½ litre	plain low-fat yogurt	16 fl oz
4 tbsp	fresh lime juice	4 tbsp
6 tbsp	amaretto liqueur	6 tbsp
	Almond cream	
35 cl	semi-skimmed milk	12 fl oz
4	egg whites	4
12.5 cl	double cream	4 fl oz
4 tbsp	caster sugar	4 tbsp
½ tsp	pure vanilla extract	½ tsp
⅛ tsp	almond extract	⅛ tsp
2 tbsp	amaretto liqueur	2 tbsp
2	limes, thinly sliced, for garnish	2

To prepare the timbales, sprinkle the gelatine over 4 tablespoons of water in a cup and let it soften for 5 minutes. Purée all but eight of the blackberries in a food processor or a blender. Strain the purée into a

heavy-bottomed non-reactive saucepan. Stir the sugar, salt and softened gelatine into the purée. Warm the purée over low heat, stirring occasionally, until the gelatine and sugar dissolve — 2 to 3 minutes. Transfer the purée to a bowl.

In another bowl, whisk together the yogurt, lime juice and amaretto. Pour this mixture into the blackberry purée, whisking constantly. Tap the bottom of the bowl on the work surface to collapse any large air bubbles, then spoon the mixture into eight fluted timbale moulds or individual jelly moulds. Refrigerate the timbales until they have set — about 2 hours.

While the timbales are chilling, prepare the almond cream. Bring ¼ litre (8 fl oz) of the milk to the boil in a clean heavy-bottomed saucepan, then immediately remove the pan from the heat. Whisk the egg whites in a clean bowl until they are frothy. Add the cream, the sugar and the remaining unheated milk. Whisking constantly, slowly pour the hot milk into the egg white mixture in a thin, steady stream; pouring slowly keeps the egg whites from forming clumps.

Return the mixture to the saucepan in which you heated the milk. Stirring constantly, thicken the sauce over medium heat until it coats the back of the spoon — 4 to 5 minutes. Remove the saucepan from the heat; stir in the vanilla and almond extracts and amaretto. Transfer the sauce to a bowl. Lay a sheet of plastic film directly on the surface of the sauce to prevent its forming a skin, and put the sauce into the ▶

refrigerator until it is chilled — about 2 hours.

To unmould a timbale, briefly dip the bottom of the mould in warm water. Invert a dessert plate over the mould, then turn the two over together, and lift away the mould. Repeat the process to unmould the other timbales. Spoon some of the sauce round each timbale and garnish each plate with a slice of lime and one of the reserved blackberries.

Spiced Pumpkin Mousse with Lemon Cream

Serves 6
Working time: about 30 minutes
Total time: about 2 hours (includes chilling)

Calories **140**
Protein **4g**
Cholesterol **18mg**
Total fat **5g**
Saturated fat **3g**
Sodium **90mg**

2½ tsp	powdered gelatine	2½ tsp
6 tbsp	caster sugar	6 tbsp
2 tsp	grated lemon rind	2 tsp
¾ tsp	aniseeds, finely ground	¾ tsp
⅛ tsp	grated nutmeg	⅛ tsp
1 tbsp	finely chopped crystallized ginger	1 tbsp
⅛ tsp	salt	⅛ tsp
250 g	canned pumpkin	8 oz
4 tbsp	fresh lemon juice	4 tbsp
4	egg whites, at room temperature	4
⅛ tsp	cream of tartar	⅛ tsp
Lemon cream		
25 g	lemon rind, julienned	¾ oz
2 tbsp	caster sugar	2 tbsp
2 tbsp	fresh lemon juice	2 tbsp
6 tbsp	double cream	6 tbsp

Put 4 tablespoons of cold water into a bowl, then sprinkle in the gelatine. Let the gelatine soften for 5 minutes; pour in 4 tablespoons of boiling water and stir to dissolve the gelatine. Stir in the sugar, lemon rind, ground aniseeds, nutmeg, ginger and salt. Add the pumpkin and lemon juice, and stir to combine them. Chill the mixture in the refrigerator, stirring occasionally, until it starts to gel — about 30 minutes.

When the pumpkin mixture is ready, beat the egg whites with the cream of tartar in a bowl until they form stiff peaks. Remove the pumpkin mixture from the refrigerator and whisk vigorously for 15 seconds. Stir in one third of the egg whites and combine them thoroughly, then fold in the remaining egg whites (*box, opposite*).

Divide the mousse into six portions, mounding each one in the centre, and chill them for 1 to 6 hours.

For the lemon cream, first put the rind in a small, non-reactive saucepan with 4 tablespoons of water, the 2 tablespoons of sugar and the 2 tablespoons of lemon juice. Bring the liquid to the boil, then reduce the heat to low, and simmer the mixture until it becomes a thick syrup — about 5 minutes. Strain the syrup into a small bowl, reserving the rind. Set half of the cooked rind aside; finely chop the rest.

Just before serving, whip the cream in a small bowl. Fold in the syrup and the finely chopped lemon rind. Garnish each mousse with a dollop of the lemon cream and a few strands of the reserved julienned rind.

Folding Mixtures Together

1 *LIGHTENING THE MIXTURE. To ensure an airy dessert's lightness, add one quarter to one third of the lighter mixture (here, beaten egg whites) to the heavier one (in this instance, pumpkin purée) and whisk them gently together. This will lighten the mixture enough so that the remaining egg whites can be folded in easily.*

2 *ADDING THE EGG WHITES. Scoop the remaining beaten egg whites into the bowl containing the lightened mixture. With a rubber spatula, cut down through the centre.*

3 *FOLDING. Glide the spatula across the bottom of the bowl, then lift and turn over the purée and egg whites as you reach the edge. Give the bowl a quarter turn. Continue cutting, lifting and turning the mixture, rotating the bowl each time, until the egg whites have been evenly incorporated.*

Indian Pudding with Buttermilk Cream

Serves 8
Working time: about 25 minutes
Total time: about 2 hours

Calories **230**
Protein **8g**
Cholesterol **13mg**
Total fat **3g**
Saturated fat **2g**
Sodium **125mg**

90 g	yellow cornmeal	3 oz
1 tsp	ground cinnamon	1 tsp
1 tsp	ground ginger	1 tsp
1 litre	semi-skimmed milk	1¾ pints
165 g	molasses	5½ oz
1 tsp	pure vanilla extract	1 tsp
Buttermilk cream		
2 tbsp	cornflour	2 tbsp
4 tbsp	sugar	4 tbsp
¼ litre	semi-skimmed milk	8 fl oz
¼ litre	buttermilk	8 fl oz
1 tsp	pure vanilla extract	1 tsp

Preheat the oven to 170°C (325°F or Mark 3).

Combine the cornmeal, cinnamon, ginger and ¼ litre (8 fl oz) of the milk in a heatproof bowl. Pour the remaining milk into a saucepan and bring it to the boil. Stirring constantly, pour the hot milk into the cornmeal mixture in a thin, steady stream.

Transfer the cornmeal mixture to the saucepan; stirring continuously, bring it to the boil. Reduce the heat to medium low and cook the mixture, stirring constantly, until it has the consistency of a thick sauce — about 3 minutes more. Stir in the molasses and the vanilla extract, then pour the cornmeal mixture into a baking dish, and bake it until it sets — about 1 hour.

While the pudding is baking, make the buttermilk cream. Mix the cornflour and sugar in a small saucepan, then whisk in the semi-skimmed milk. Bring the mixture to the boil and cook it for 1 minute. Remove the pan from the heat and stir in the buttermilk and vanilla. Transfer the buttermilk cream to a bowl and chill it in the refrigerator.

Remove the pudding from the oven and allow it to cool at room temperature for about 45 minutes; just before serving, top the pudding with the chilled buttermilk cream.

Orange Chiffon Cheesecake

Serves 12
Working time: about 1 hour
Total time: about 1 day (includes chilling)

Calories **145**
Protein **7g**
Cholesterol **12mg**
Total fat **4g**
Saturated fat **2g**
Sodium **130mg**

200 g	sugar	7 oz
2	oranges, halved lengthwise and cut crosswise into 3mm (⅛ inch) slices	2
12.5 cl	fresh orange juice	4 fl oz
2½ tbsp	fresh lemon juice	2½ tbsp
2½ tsp	powdered gelatine	2½ tsp
250 g	low-fat ricotta cheese	8 oz
225 g	low-fat cottage cheese	7½ oz
60 g	low-fat creamy soft cheese	2 oz
1	orange, grated rind only	1
1	lemon, grated rind only	1
3	egg whites	3

Put the sugar and 12.5 cl (4 fl oz) of water into a saucepan. Bring the mixture to the boil, then add the orange slices, reduce the heat, and simmer the oranges for 20 minutes. Refrigerate the oranges in the syrup for 1 hour.

Pour the orange juice and lemon juice into a small saucepan. Sprinkle in the gelatine, then set the pan aside until the gelatine has softened.

Meanwhile, purée the ricotta, cottage cheese, soft cheese, orange rind and lemon rind in a food processor or a blender until the mixture is very smooth. Transfer the cheese mixture to a bowl.

Set the saucepan containing the gelatine mixture over low heat; cook it, stirring continuously, until the gelatine has dissolved. Stir the gelatine mixture into the puréed cheeses.

Remove the orange slices from their syrup and drain them on paper towels. Reserve the syrup.

Pour the egg whites into a deep bowl. Set up an electric mixer; you will need to start beating the egg whites as soon as the syrup is ready.

To prepare Italian meringue *(page 95),* heat the

reserved syrup in a small saucepan over medium-high heat until it boils. Continue to boil the mixture until the bubbles rise to the surface in a random pattern, indicating that the liquid has nearly evaporated and the sugar itself is beginning to cook.

With a small spoon, drop a little of the syrup into a bowl filled with iced water. If the syrup dissolves immediately, continue cooking the syrup mixture. When the syrup dropped into the water can be rolled between your fingers into a supple ball, begin beating the egg whites on high speed. Pour the syrup down the side of the bowl in a very thin, steady stream. When all the syrup has been incorporated, decrease the speed to medium; continue beating the egg whites until they are glossy, have formed stiff peaks and have cooled to room temperature. Increase the speed to high and beat the meringue for 1 minute more.

Mix about one quarter of the meringue into the cheese mixture to lighten it, then gently fold in the rest *(page 103)*. Rinse a 1.5 litre (2½ pint) ring mould with cold water and shake out the excess. (Do not wipe the mould dry; the clinging moisture will help the dessert unmould cleanly.) Line the mould with the drained orange slices, then pour in the cheesecake mixture, and chill it in the refrigerator for 4 hours.

To turn out the cheesecake, invert a chilled platter on top of the mould and turn both over together. Wrap the bottom of the mould in a towel that has been soaked with hot water and wrung out. After 5 seconds, remove the towel and lift away the mould.

Kugel with Dried Fruit

Serves 12
Working time: about 35 minutes
Total time: about 1 hour and 35 minutes

Calories **325**
Protein **13g**
Cholesterol **17mg**
Total fat **6g**
Saturated fat **3g**
Sodium **230mg**

250 g	dried wide egg noodles	8 oz
200 g	sugar	7 oz
500 g	low-fat cottage cheese	1 lb
250 g	curd cheese	8 oz
¼ litre	plain low-fat yogurt	8 fl oz
1 tsp	pure vanilla extract	1 tsp
2 tbsp	fresh lemon juice	2 tbsp
150 g	sultanas	5 oz
75 g	dried pears, diced	2½ oz
60 g	dried apples, diced	2 oz
75 g	dried stoned prunes, diced	2½ oz
2 tbsp	cornflour	2 tbsp
½ litre	semi-skimmed milk	16 fl oz
2 tbsp	dry breadcrumbs	2 tbsp
Cinnamon topping		
30 g	unsalted butter, softened	1 oz
60 g	dry breadcrumbs	2 oz
½ tsp	ground cinnamon	½ tsp
2 tbsp	sugar	2 tbsp

Add the noodles to 3 litres (5 pints) of boiling water. Start testing for doneness after 7 minutes and continue cooking the noodles until they are *al dente*. Drain the noodles and rinse them under cold running water, then set them aside.

Preheat the oven to 180°C (350°F or Mark 4). In a large bowl, mix together the sugar, cottage cheese, curd cheese, yogurt, vanilla extract, lemon juice, sultanas, pears, apples and prunes. Dissolve the cornflour in 12.5 cl (4 fl oz) of the milk. Stir the cornflour mixture and the remaining milk into the cheese mixture.

Stir the noodles together with the cheese mixture, coating them well. Lightly oil a non-reactive 23 by 33 cm (9 by 13 inch) baking dish and coat it with the two tablespoons of breadcrumbs. Transfer the noodles to the baking dish.

To make the cinnamon topping, mix together the butter, the breadcrumbs, the cinnamon and the sugar. Sprinkle the topping over the noodles, then cover the dish with foil, and bake it for 30 minutes. Remove the foil and bake the kugel until it is golden-brown — about 30 minutes more.

4

Dessert Cakes and Assemblies

With a knowing choice of ingredients and with the right preparation techniques, pies, pastries and cakes that are ordinarily laden with fat and calories can be brought within the bounds of healthy eating. What is more, this can be accomplished without sacrificing the flavours that make such confections so appealing. Two staples of traditional dessert cookery — butter and egg yolks — have a place in the doughs and batters in this section, but they form a relatively small proportion of a recipe's total ingredients. Although the dough for profiteroles has in the past been made with whole eggs, replacing some of the egg yolks with egg whites, it turns out, still produces a light and billowing puff *(page 113)*.

The familiar white wheat flour figures in many of the following recipes, but others incorporate flours and grains with greater nutritional value. Wholemeal flour lends an earthy undertone and added fibre to orange beetroot cake, a variation on carrot cake and courgette bread. The dessert crêpes on page 108 feature high-protein buckwheat flour. When fruit is used, as in the apple-rhubarb pastries on page 117 or the lemon corn-meal cake with blueberry sauce on page 120, there can be a bonus of vitamins, minerals and fibre.

Some of the 18 desserts in this section are based on stiffly beaten egg whites and sugar, which, of course, contain no fat at all. Among these are the crisply baked, snow-white meringue baskets on page 124, ideal for filling with fresh fruit. Beaten egg whites also leaven three kinds of cake — angel food, sponge and chiffon — presented here in new guises. After beating the whites to the desired consistency, finish the recipe promptly and transfer the dessert to the oven without delay; if allowed to stand, the egg white foam would begin to dry out and lose its flexibility.

Apple-Filled Buckwheat Crêpes with Apple Syrup

Serves 4
Working time: about 1 hour
Total time: about 1 hour and 30 minutes

Calories **320**
Protein **4g**
Cholesterol **70mg**
Total fat **11g**
Saturated fat **2g**
Sodium **95mg**

½ litre	unsweetened apple juice	16 fl oz
500 g	sweet apples	1 lb
¼ tsp	ground cinnamon	¼ tsp
2 tbsp	soured cream	2 tbsp
Crêpe batter		
25 g	buckwheat flour	¾ oz
75 g	plain flour	2½ oz
⅛ tsp	salt	⅛ tsp
1	egg	1
2 tbsp	plus ¼ tsp safflower oil	2 tbsp

To prepare the crêpe batter, sift together the buckwheat flour, plain flour and salt. In a large bowl, whisk together the egg, 2 tablespoons of the oil and 4 tablespoons of water. Gradually whisk in the sifted ingredients until a smooth mixture results. Cover the bowl and refrigerate the batter for at least 1 hour.

Bring 35 cl (12 fl oz) of the apple juice to the boil in a heavy-bottomed saucepan. Lower the heat to medium low and boil the juice until it is reduced to 4 tablespoons — 20 to 30 minutes. Set the apple syrup aside.

Peel, quarter and core the apples, then cut the quarters into 1 cm (½ inch) pieces. Combine the apple pieces with the cinnamon and the remaining apple juice in a large, shallow, heavy-bottomed pan set over medium heat. Cook the apple mixture, stirring occasionally, until almost all of the liquid has evaporated — 15 to 20 minutes. Transfer the apple mixture to a food processor or a blender, and purée it. Return the purée to the pan and keep it in a warm place.

When the batter is chilled, heat a crêpe pan or a 20 cm (8 inch) frying pan over medium-high heat. Pour in the remaining ¼ teaspoon of oil; with a paper towel, wipe the oil over the pan's entire cooking surface. Pour 2 to 3 tablespoons of the crêpe batter into the hot pan and immediately swirl the pan to coat the bottom with a thin, even layer of batter. Pour any excess batter back into the bowl. Cook the crêpe until the bottom is browned — about 2½ minutes — then lift the edge with a spatula and turn the crêpe over. Cook the crêpe on the second side until it too is browned — 15 to 30 seconds — and slide the crêpe on to a warmed plate. Repeat the process with the remaining batter to form eight crêpes in all.

Spread about 3 tablespoons of the warm apple purée over each crêpe. Fold each crêpe in half, then fold it in half again to produce a wedge shape. Arrange two crêpes, one slightly overlapping the other, on each of four dessert plates. Dribble a tablespoon of the apple syrup over each serving; garnish each dessert with ½ tablespoon of the soured cream and serve at once.

Bananas and Oranges in Chocolate Puffs

Serves 16
Working time: about 45 minutes
Total time: about 1 hour and 45 minutes

Calories **160**
Protein **5g**
Cholesterol **60mg**
Total fat **6g**
Saturated fat **2g**
Sodium **70mg**

150 g	plain flour	5 oz
1 tbsp	unsweetened cocoa powder	1 tbsp
1 tsp	ground cinnamon	1 tsp
½ tsp	grated nutmeg	½ tsp
30 g	unsalted butter	1 oz
2 tbsp	safflower oil	2 tbsp
¼ tsp	salt	¼ tsp
2 tbsp	caster sugar	2 tbsp
3	eggs, plus 2 egg whites	3
4	ripe bananas	4
4	oranges, segmented (page 14)	4
Ricotta filling		
225 g	low-fat ricotta cheese	7½ oz
2 tbsp	caster sugar	2 tbsp
1 tsp	pure vanilla extract	1 tsp
2 tbsp	icing sugar	2 tbsp

Mix together the flour, cocoa powder, cinnamon and nutmeg; set the mixture aside. Preheat the oven to 200°C (400°F or Mark 6).

Combine the butter, oil, salt, sugar and ¼ litre (8 fl oz) of water in a saucepan, and bring the mixture to the boil. As soon as the butter melts, remove the pan from the heat and stir in the flour mixture with a wooden spoon. Return the pan to the stove over medium heat and cook the mixture, stirring vigorously, until it comes cleanly away from the sides of the pan.

Remove the pan from the heat once more and allow it to cool for 2 minutes before adding the eggs. Incorporate the whole eggs one at a time, beating vigorously after you add each one, until the dough is smooth. In a separate bowl, whisk the egg whites until they are frothy; beat half of the egg whites into the dough. To test the consistency of the dough, scoop some up with a spoon, then turn the spoon and wait for the dough to fall off; it should fall off cleanly at the count of three. If it does not, beat in more of the egg whites and repeat the test.

Spoon the dough into a piping bag fitted with a 1 cm (½ inch) star nozzle. Pipe the dough on to a lightly oiled baking sheet in mounting swirls about 4 cm (1½ inches) across. (If you do not have a piping bag, fashion 4 cm/1½ inch mounds with a spoon.) Bake the puffs until they expand and are firm to the touch — about 25 minutes. Turn off the oven, prop the door ajar with a wooden spoon, and let the puffs dry in the oven for 15 minutes. Then transfer them to a rack to cool.

While the puffs are cooling, make the filling: purée the ricotta in a food processor or a blender, then blend in the sugar and vanilla. Refrigerate the filling.

To assemble the dessert, cut each puff in half horizontally. Fill the lower halves with the chilled ricotta mixture. Peel the bananas and slice them into rounds; then arrange the banana rounds and orange segments on top of the filling. Replace the upper halves of the puffs. Sift the icing sugar over all, and serve the puffs at once.

Apple Gateau

Serves 8
Working time: about 40 minutes
Total time: about 4 hours (includes chilling)

Calories **200**
Protein **4g**
Cholesterol **5mg**
Total fat **2g**
Saturated fat **0g**
Sodium **180mg**

1 kg	cooking apples, peeled, cored and sliced	2½ lb
90 g	granulated sugar	3 oz
2	lemons, rind finely grated, juice of 1 strained	2
250 g	breadcrumbs	8 oz
2 tsp	freshly ground cinnamon	2 tsp
90 g	demerara sugar	3 oz
2 tsp	icing sugar	2 tsp
1	small red apple, cored, halved, cut into thin slices and brushed with lemon juice to prevent discoloration	1
150 g	thick Greek yogurt	5 oz

Put the cooking apples, granulated sugar, half the grated lemon rind and the lemon juice in a large saucepan. Cover with a tightly fitting lid and cook over a gentle heat until the apples are soft and fluffy. Pour the cooked apples into a large nylon sieve, and place the sieve over a bowl, to drain and cool.

Meanwhile, heat the oven to 200°C (400°F or Mark 6). Mix the breadcrumbs with the cinnamon and demerara sugar; spread the crumbs out in a thin layer on a large baking sheet. Brown them in the oven for about 20 minutes, stirring frequently with a fork to prevent the crumbs sticking together.

Reduce the heat to 180°C (350°F or Mark 4). Lightly oil a 20 cm (8 inch) springform tin, or loose-based cake tin; line the base with a round of non-stick parchment paper. Spread one third of the crumbs in the bottom of the tin, then spread half of the cooked apples evenly over the crumbs. Add half the remaining crumbs and then the remaining apples. Sprinkle the rest of the crumbs evenly over the top, pressing them down lightly. Bake for 35 minutes. Remove from the oven, allow to cool, then refrigerate until cold.

Carefully transfer the gateau from the tin to a serving plate. Sift 1 teaspoon of the icing sugar over the top, and decorate with the red apple slices. Mix the yogurt with the remaining icing sugar and lemon rind, and serve in a separate dish.

Honey-Glazed Buttermilk Cake

Serves 16
Working time: about 30 minutes
Total time: about 2 hours and 30 minutes

Calories **310**
Protein **6g**
Cholesterol **10mg**
Total fat **6g**
Saturated fat **3g**
Sodium **190mg**

375 g	plain flour	13 oz
1 tsp	bicarbonate of soda	1 tsp
450 g	caster sugar	15 oz
60 g	unsalted butter, cut into 1 cm (½ inch) pats	2 oz
60 g	polyunsaturated margarine	2 oz
2 tsp	pure vanilla extract	2 tsp
35 cl	buttermilk	12 fl oz
4	egg whites	4
1	lemon, grated rind only	1
Honey glaze		
4 tbsp	sugar	4 tbsp
4 tbsp	buttermilk	4 tbsp
90 g	honey	3 oz
½ tsp	pure vanilla extract	½ tsp

Grease a 3 litre (5 pint) kugelhopf mould and dust it with flour. Preheat the oven to 170°C (325°F or Mark 3).

Mix the flour, bicarbonate of soda and sugar in a bowl. With an electric mixer on the lowest speed, cut the butter and margarine into the dry ingredients until the mixture has the consistency of fine meal.

Stir together the vanilla extract, buttermilk and egg whites. Mix half of this liquid with the dry ingredients on medium-low speed for 1 minute. Add the remaining liquid and mix it in at medium speed for 1 minute more, scraping down the sides of the bowl as necessary. Stir in the grated lemon rind.

Pour the batter into the prepared mould. Bake the cake until it begins to pull away from the sides of the mould and feels springy to the touch — about 55 minutes. Set the cake aside to cool in the mould.

To make the glaze, combine the sugar, buttermilk and honey in a small saucepan. Bring the liquid to the boil over medium heat, then continue boiling it, stirring occasionally, until it is a light caramel colour and has thickened slightly — about 10 minutes. (Although the buttermilk in the glaze will separate when the liquid first comes to the boil, the subsequent cooking will yield a smooth, well-blended sauce.)

Remove the saucepan from the heat; stir in the vanilla extract and 1 teaspoon of water. Let the mixture cool completely — it should be thick enough to coat the back of a spoon. Invert the cooled cake on to a serving platter. Lift away the mould and pour the glaze over the cake, letting the glaze run down the sides.

Orange-Beetroot Cake

Serves 16
Working time: about 1 hour
Total time: about 1 hour and 45 minutes

Calories **190**
Protein **3g**
Cholesterol **50mg**
Total fat **6g**
Saturated fat **1g**
Sodium **115mg**

45 g	sultanas	1½ oz
45 g	raisins	1½ oz
¼ litre	fresh orange juice	8 fl oz
100 g	plain flour	3½ oz
90 g	wholemeal flour	3 oz
1 tsp	bicarbonate of soda	1 tsp
¼ tsp	salt	¼ tsp
1 tsp	ground cinnamon	1 tsp
1 tsp	grated nutmeg	1 tsp
3	eggs, separated, the whites at room temperature	3
6 tbsp	safflower oil	6 tbsp
1 tbsp	grated orange rind	1 tbsp
1 tsp	pure vanilla extract	1 tsp
75 g	dark brown sugar	2½ oz
6 tbsp	plain low-fat yogurt	6 tbsp
3	raw beetroots, peeled and grated	3
135 g	caster sugar	4½ oz

Put the sultanas, raisins and orange juice into a non-reactive saucepan. Bring the juice to the boil, then reduce the heat and simmer the mixture for 5 minutes. Drain the sultanas and raisins in a sieve set over another non-reactive saucepan; reserve the juice and set the sultanas and raisins aside. Return the juice to the heat and simmer it until only about 3 table-spoons remain — 7 minutes or so.

Preheat the oven to 180°C (350°F or Mark 4).

Lightly oil a 23 cm (9 inch) springform tin. Line the base of the tin with a disc of greaseproof paper, then lightly oil the paper, and dust the tin with flour.

Sift the plain flour, wholemeal flour, bicarbonate of soda, salt, cinnamon and nutmeg into a bowl. In a separate bowl, whisk the egg yolks. Stir 1 tablespoon of the oil into the yolks. Whisking vigorously, blend in the remaining oil a tablespoon at a time. Continue whisking the yolks until the mixture is emulsified. Stir the orange rind, vanilla extract, brown sugar, yogurt, beetroot, sultanas and raisins into the yolk mixture. Fold the flour mixture into the yolk mixture.

Beat the egg whites until soft peaks form. Sprinkle in the caster sugar and beat for 1 minute more. Stir one quarter of the beaten egg whites into the batter to lighten it, then gently fold the lightened batter into the remaining beaten egg whites. Pour the batter mixture into the prepared springform tin.

Bake the cake just until a knife inserted in the centre comes out clean — 45 to 55 minutes. Remove the cake from the oven and let it cool for 10 minutes. Gently reheat the reserved orange juice and brush it over the top of the warm cake.

EDITOR'S NOTE: *This cake tastes even better two or three days after it has been baked. Store it in an airtight container.*

Cherry Puffs

Serves 12
Working time: about 1 hour and 10 minutes
Total time: about 2 hours

Calories **170**
Protein **5g**
Cholesterol **75mg**
Total fat **7g**
Saturated fat **2g**
Sodium **80mg**

750 g	sweet cherries, stoned	1½ lb
4	lemons, grated rind only	4
12.5 cl	fresh lemon juice	4 fl oz
2 tbsp	cornflour	2 tbsp
4 tbsp	kirsch	4 tbsp
17.5 cl	plain low-fat yogurt	6 fl oz
2 tbsp	caster sugar	2 tbsp
Choux paste		
30 g	unsalted butter	1 oz
2 tbsp	safflower oil	2 tbsp
¼ tsp	salt	¼ tsp
1 tsp	caster sugar	1 tsp
150 g	plain flour	5 oz
3	eggs, plus 2 egg whites	3

Combine the cherries, lemon rind and lemon juice in a saucepan over medium-high heat. Bring the mixture to the boil, then reduce the heat to maintain a simmer, and cook the mixture for 5 minutes. Combine the cornflour with the kirsch in a small bowl and stir them into the cherry mixture. Continue cooking, stirring constantly, until the mixture thickens — about 2 minutes. Set the cherry filling aside at room temperature.

Whisk together the yogurt and sugar in a small bowl; refrigerate the bowl.

Preheat the oven to 220°C (425°F or Mark 7).

To make the choux paste, combine the butter, oil, salt, sugar and ¼ litre (8 fl oz) of water in a heavy-bottomed saucepan. Bring the mixture to the boil over medium-high heat. As soon as the butter melts, remove the pan from the heat and stir in the flour with a wooden spoon. Return the pan to the stove over medium heat; cook the mixture, stirring constantly, until it comes cleanly away from the sides of the pan and leaves a slight film on the bottom.

Remove the pan from the heat once more and allow it to cool for 2 minutes before adding the eggs. Incorporate the eggs one at a time, beating well after you add each one, until a smooth dough results. In a separate bowl, whisk the egg whites until they are frothy; beat one half of the egg whites into the dough. To test the consistency of the dough, scoop some up with a spoon, then turn the spoon and wait for the dough to fall off; it should fall off cleanly at the count of three. If it does not, beat more of the egg whites into the dough.

Spoon the dough into a piping bag fitted with a 1 cm (½ inch) plain nozzle. Pipe the dough on to a lightly oiled baking sheet in 12 mounting swirls about 5 cm (2 inches) in diameter and 5 cm (2 inches) apart. (If you do not have a piping bag, fashion the swirls with a spoon.) Bake the swirls until they puff up and are uniformly browned — about 25 minutes. Turn off the oven, prop the door ajar with the handle of a wooden spoon, and let the puffs dry in the oven for 15 minutes. Transfer the puffs to a rack to cool.

To assemble the puffs, slice each in half horizontally and spoon the cherry filling into the bottoms. Top each filling with a tablespoon of the sweetened yogurt; replace the tops and serve the puffs immediately.

Marbled Angel Food Cake

Serves 12
Working time: about 25 minutes
Total time: about 2 hours and 30 minutes

Calories **130**
Protein **4g**
Cholesterol **0mg**
Total fat **0g**
Saturated fat **0g**
Sodium **65mg**

100 g	plain flour	3½ oz
3 tbsp	unsweetened cocoa powder	3 tbsp
250 g	caster sugar	8 oz
⅛ tsp	salt	⅛ tsp
10	egg whites	10
1 tsp	cream of tartar	1 tsp
½ tsp	almond extract	½ tsp
½ tsp	pure vanilla extract	½ tsp
1 tbsp	icing sugar	1 tbsp

Sift 5 tablespoons of the flour, the cocoa powder and 2 tablespoons of the sugar into a bowl. Sift the cocoa mixture three more times and set the bowl aside. Sift the remaining flour, the salt and 2 tablespoons of the remaining sugar into a second bowl. Sift this mixture three more times and set it aside too.

Preheat the oven to 180°C (350°F or Mark 4). Rinse out a tube cake tin and shake — do not wipe — it dry.

With an electric mixer, beat the egg whites until soft peaks form when the beater is lifted. Add the cream of tartar, then blend in the remaining sugar a little at a time, beating the egg whites until they form stiff peaks. With the mixer set on the lowest speed, blend in the almond extract, then the vanilla extract. Transfer half of the beaten egg whites to a clean bowl.

Fold the dry cocoa mixture into the beaten egg whites in one bowl, then pour this chocolate batter into the tube tin. Fold the remaining dry mixture into the beaten egg whites in the other bowl, and spoon the batter over the chocolate batter in the tube tin. Plunge a spatula down through both layers of batter, then bring it back to the surface with a twisting motion. Repeat this step at 2.5 cm (1 inch) intervals round the cake to marble the batter thoroughly.

Bake the cake for 45 minutes. Invert the tin and let the cake cool for 90 minutes. Run a knife round the sides of the tin to loosen the cake before turning it out. Sift the icing sugar over the cake.

Chocolate Chiffon Cake with Raspberry Filling

Serves 12
Working time: about 40 minutes
Total time: about 2 hours

Calories **205**
Protein **3g**
Cholesterol **45mg**
Total fat **6g**
Saturated fat **1g**
Sodium **110mg**

4 tbsp	unsweetened cocoa powder	4 tbsp
100 g	plain flour	3½ oz
150 g	caster sugar	5 oz
1 tsp	bicarbonate of soda	1 tsp
⅛ tsp	salt	⅛ tsp
4 tbsp	safflower oil	4 tbsp
2	eggs, separated, plus 2 egg whites, the whites at room temperature	2
1 tsp	pure vanilla extract	1 tsp
¼ tsp	cream of tartar	¼ tsp
Raspberry filling		
250 g	fresh or frozen raspberries	8 oz
100 g	sugar	3½ oz
Raspberry-champagne sauce		
250 g	fresh or frozen raspberries, thawed	8 oz
½ tsp	fresh lemon juice	½ tsp
17.5 cl	chilled dry champagne (¼-bottle)	6 fl oz
2 tbsp	caster sugar (if you are using fresh raspberries)	2 tbsp

Spoon the cocoa powder into a small heatproof bowl and stir in 12.5 cl (4 fl oz) of boiling water. Set the bowl aside. Preheat the oven to 180°C (350°F or Mark 4).

Sift the flour, half the caster sugar, the bicarbonate of soda and salt into a large bowl. Stir in the oil, egg yolks, the cocoa mixture and the vanilla; mix to blend the ingredients.

Pour the egg whites into a bowl and beat them until they are frothy. Add the cream of tartar, then continue beating the whites until soft peaks form. Gradually adding the remaining sugar, beat the whites until they form stiff peaks. Mix one third of the beaten whites into the flour mixture to lighten it; gently fold in the remaining whites. Pour the mixture into a 23 by 12.5 by 7.5 cm (9 by 5 by 3 inch) loaf tin. Bake the cake until a wooden toothpick inserted in the centre comes out clean — about 55 minutes. Invert the tin on a cake rack and let the cake cool completely.

While the cake is cooling, make the raspberry filling. ▶

Combine the raspberries, sugar and 2 tablespoons of water in a heavy saucepan over medium heat; cook the mixture, stirring constantly, until it has the consistency of jam — about 25 minutes. Refrigerate the filling.

For the sauce, purée the raspberries with the lemon juice in a food processor or a blender. (If you are using fresh raspberries, include the 2 tablespoons of sugar in the purée.) Strain the purée into a bowl; discard the solids. Refrigerate the purée.

Run a knife blade round the sides of the loaf tin, then invert the tin again and rap it sharply against the work surface to unmould the cake. Cut the cake into two horizontal layers. Spread the chilled raspberry filling over the bottom layer, then set the top layer back in place. Just before serving, stir the champagne into the chilled raspberry purée. Cut the cake into serving slices, and surround each one with a little of the raspberry-champagne sauce.

Papaya Porcupines with Coconut Quills

Makes about 20 porcupines
Working time: about 30 minutes
Total time: about 45 minutes

Per porcupine:
Calories **50**
Protein **1g**
Cholesterol **0mg**
Total fat **1g**
Saturated fat **1g**
Sodium **14mg**

2	egg whites	2
2 tbsp	fresh lemon juice	2 tbsp
75 g	plain flour	2½ oz
6 tbsp	caster sugar	6 tbsp
60 g	shredded coconut	2 oz
1	papaya (about 500 g/1 lb), peeled and cut into about 20 chunks	1

Preheat the oven to 200°C (400°F or Mark 6).

Prepare the coating for the papaya: in a small bowl, thoroughly whisk the egg whites, lemon juice, flour and 2 tablespoons of the sugar. Set aside. Spread out the coconut on a sheet of greaseproof paper.

Toss the papaya pieces with the remaining sugar. Dip a piece of papaya into the coating, then hold the piece over the bowl and allow the excess coating to drip off. Roll the papaya piece in the coconut, then transfer it to a baking sheet. Repeat the process to coat the remaining pieces.

Bake the papaya porcupines until the coating has set and is lightly browned — about 15 minutes. Serve the papaya porcupines warm.

Rhubarb Tartlets Topped with Meringue

Serves 4

Working (and total) time: about 1 hour and 30 minutes

Calories **200**
Protein **3g**
Cholesterol **7mg**
Total fat **5g**
Saturated fat **2g**
Sodium **180mg**

1	tart green apple, peeled, cored and cut into 1 cm (½ inch) cubes	1
2 tbsp	dry white wine	2 tbsp
500 g	fresh rhubarb, trimmed and cut into 1 cm (½ inch) pieces, or frozen rhubarb, thawed	1 lb
4 tbsp	light brown sugar	4 tbsp
¼ tsp	pure vanilla extract	¼ tsp
½ tsp	fresh lemon juice	½ tsp
¼ tsp	ground cinnamon	¼ tsp
	grated nutmeg	
⅛ tsp	salt	⅛ tsp
4	sheets frozen phyllo (minimum width 25 cm/10 inches) in a stack, thawed	4
15 g	unsalted butter, melted	½ oz
1	egg white	1
1½ tbsp	caster sugar	1½ tbsp

Put the apple cubes and wine into a saucepan and simmer them, covered, for 5 minutes. Add the rhubarb, reduce the heat to low, and cook the mixture, uncovered, for 5 minutes more. Stir in the brown sugar, vanilla, lemon juice, cinnamon, a pinch of nutmeg and the salt. Continue cooking the mixture, stirring occasionally, until most of the liquid has evaporated — 5 to 10 minutes. Set the mixture aside.

Preheat the oven to 180°C (350°F or Mark 4).

To prepare the pastry, fold the stack of phyllo sheets in half, then fold it in half again and trim off the edges so as to produce a stack of sixteen 12.5 cm (5 inch) squares. Lay one of the phyllo squares on a work surface; using a pastry brush, lightly dab the square with a little of the melted butter. Set a second square on top of the first and brush it with butter. Set a third square on top of the second at a 45-degree angle, forming an eight-pointed star. Dab the top of the third square with butter and cover it with a fourth square.

Lightly oil four cups of a muffin tin. Transfer the stacked phyllo to one of the cups and gently press it in place, taking care that the edges of the phyllo come as far as possible up the sides of the cup. Prepare the remaining phyllo squares in the same manner, making four tartlets in all.

Bake the tartlets until they are light brown and crisp — about 8 minutes. Remove the muffin tin from the oven and unmould the tartlets, then set them aside. Let the tartlets cool to room temperature.

Increase the oven temperature to 240°C (475°F or Mark 9).

To make the meringue, beat the egg white in a small bowl until the white forms soft peaks. Continue beating, gradually adding the sugar, until stiff peaks form when the beater is lifted from the bowl.

Set the tartlets on a baking sheet and divide the rhubarb mixture among them. Using a piping bag or a spoon, top each with some of the meringue; bake the tartlets until the meringue browns — about 3 minutes. Serve the tartlets within 2 hours.

Greek Yogurt Flan

Serves 8
Working time: about 40 minutes
Total time: about 3 hours (includes chilling)

Calories **115**
Protein **3g**
Cholesterol **60mg**
Total fat **3g**
Saturated fat **1g**
Sodium **40mg**

2	eggs	
1	egg white	
90 g	caster sugar	3
90 g	plain flour	3
250 g	thick Greek yogurt	8
1 tbsp	sifted icing sugar	1 tb.
1	orange, finely grated rind only	
3 tbsp	orange juice mixed with 3 tbsp cointreau	3 tb.
8	fresh ripe figs, each cut into 8 pieces, skin removed if bitter	

Heat the oven to 180°C (350°F or Mark 4). Butter
22 cm (10 inch) fluted sponge flan tin. Put the egg
egg white and sugar into a large bowl and prepa
the sponge mixture as shown below. Pour the mixtu
into the prepared tin and spread it evenly. Bake f
25 minutes, until very lightly browned and springy t
the touch. Turn out on to a wire rack to cool.

Put one third of the yogurt into a piping bag fitte
with a star nozzle and refrigerate until needed. Mix th
remaining yogurt with the icing sugar and the fine
grated orange rind.

Place the sponge flan on a serving dish. Spoon th
orange juice and cointreau evenly over the centre
the flan, then spread the orange-flavoured yogurt
top. Pipe a decorative border round the edge with th
yogurt in the piping bag. Arrange the fig pieces on th
yogurt in the centre. Cover loosely with plastic film an
chill in the refrigerator for 1 hour before serving.

Making a Fat-Free Sponge

1 CREAMING THE EGGS AND SUGAR.
Beat the eggs, egg white and sugar
with an electric mixer for 6 to 8
minutes. The mixture should be creamy
and fall off the whisk in a thick ribbon.

2 INCORPORATING THE FLOUR. Sift the flour on to the top of the
mixture, lightly tapping the side of the sieve with your hand (above,
left). Using a rubber spatula or large metal spoon, gently incorporate the
flour by cutting and folding it into the mixture (above, right).

3 BAKING THE SPONGE. Lightly
butter a fluted flan tin. Pour the
mixture into the tin and spread it evenly.
Bake until pale brown and springy to
the touch — about 25 minutes.

Strawberry Trifle Gateau

Serves 8
Working time: about 35 minutes
Total time: about 6 hours (includes chilling)

Calories **240**
Protein **10g**
Cholesterol **90mg**
Total fat **3g**
Saturated fat **1g**
Sodium **50mg**

3	eggs	3
1	egg white	1
200 g	caster sugar	7 oz
125 g	plain flour	4 oz
750 g	fresh strawberries 500 g (1 lb) hulled and thinly sliced, the rest reserved for decoration	1½ lb
250 g	quark	8 oz
1 tsp	pure vanilla extract	1 tsp
1 tsp	icing sugar	1 tsp
15 g	shelled pistachio nuts, skinned and thinly sliced	½ oz

Heat the oven to 180°C (350°F or Mark 4). Lightly oil a 22 cm (10 inch) springform tin or cake tin. Line the base with greaseproof paper.

Put the whole eggs and egg white into a large bowl with 125 g (4 oz) of the caster sugar and prepare the sponge mixture as demonstrated on the left. Pour the mixture into the prepared tin and spread it evenly. Bake for 25 to 30 minutes, until very lightly browned and springy to the touch. Leave the sponge to cool slightly in the tin for a few minutes, then carefully turn it out on to a wire rack to cool completely.

Meanwhile, put the sliced strawberries into a bowl with 50 g (2 oz) of the caster sugar. Mix well, cover and leave to stand for about 1½ hours, to allow the strawberries to soften and the sugar to draw out the juice. Blend the quark with the remaining sugar and vanilla.

Cut the cooled sponge in half horizontally. Place the bottom layer on a flat plate. Fit an expanding ring snugly round it (or, alternatively, a deep band of double thickness foil) in order to retain the shape. Spoon half the sliced strawberries and their juice over the sponge layer, then spread on the quark. Spoon the remaining sliced strawberries on top of the quark. Place the second sponge layer on top of the strawberries. Cover the sponge with plastic film and put a flat plate on top. Place some large weights or cans on top of the plate to weight down the gateau. Refrigerate for at least 4 hours, or overnight.

To serve, remove the weights, plate and plastic film. Carefully remove the ring. Slice the reserved strawberries, and use them to decorate the gateau. Sift on the icing sugar and sprinkle the top with the sliced pistachios. Keep refrigerated until ready to serve.

135 g (4½ oz) of the sugar, and the tangerine orange rind and juice, and mix them thoroughly.

To prepare the meringue, beat the whites and crea of tartar together in another bowl until the whites ho soft peaks. Add the remaining sugar 2 tablespoons a time, beating continuously until the whites are shir and hold stiff peaks.

Stir one third of the meringue into the cake batter lighten it, then fold in the remaining meringue. Rinse 25 cm (10 inch) kugelhopf mould or tube cake tin wi water and shake it out so that only a few drople remain. Spoon the batter into the mould and bake th cake for 50 minutes. Increase the oven temperature 180°C (350°F or Mark 4) and continue baking the ca until a skewer inserted in the thickest part comes o clean — 5 to 15 minutes more.

When the cake is done, remove it from the oven ar let it rest for 10 minutes. Loosen it from the sides of th mould with a spatula and invert it on to a rack. Allo the cake to cool completely — about 1½ hours.

To prepare the lemon glaze, first sift the icing sug into a small bowl, then stir in the lemon juice and rin Continue stirring until a smooth paste results. Stir the soured cream and pour the glaze over the cak letting the excess cascade down the sides.

Tangerine Chiffon Cake with Lemon Glaze

Serves 16
Working time: about 30 minutes
Total time: about 3 hours (includes cooling)

Calories **200**
Protein **3g**
Cholesterol **70mg**
Total fat **6g**
Saturated fat **1g**
Sodium **110mg**

250 g	plain flour	8 oz
1 tbsp	baking powder	1 tbsp
4	eggs, separated, plus 3 egg whites	4
6 tbsp	safflower oil	6 tbsp
265 g	caster sugar	8¼ oz
2½ tbsp	finely chopped tangerine rind or grated orange rind	2½ tbsp
¼ litre	strained tangerine juice or orange juice, preferably fresh	8 fl oz
½ tsp	cream of tartar	½ tsp
Lemon glaze		
90 g	icing sugar	3 oz
1 tbsp	fresh lemon juice	1 tbsp
1 tbsp	grated lemon rind	1 tbsp
1 tbsp	soured cream	1 tbsp

Preheat the oven to 170°C (325°F or Mark 3).

To make the cake batter, sift the flour and baking powder into a large bowl. Whisk in the egg yolks, oil,

Lemon Cornmeal Cake with Blueberry Sauce

Serves 10
Working time: about 35 minutes
Total time: about 1 hour and 30 minutes

Calories **215**
Protein **4g**
Cholesterol **68mg**
Total fat **9g**
Saturated fat **4g**
Sodium **90mg**

2 tbsp	desiccated coconut	2 tb
100 g	caster sugar	3½
30 g	blanched almonds	1
125 g	cornmeal	4
70 g	plain flour	2½
1½ tsp	baking powder	1½ t
12.5 cl	buttermilk	4 fl
1	lemon, grated rind and juice	
60 g	unsalted butter	2
2	eggs	
300 g	blueberries	10
⅛ tsp	ground cinnamon	⅛ t

Preheat the oven to 180°C (350°F or Mark 4). C pieces of greaseproof paper to fit the bottom and side of a 23 by 12.5 cm (9 by 5 inch) loaf tin. Line the t with the greaseproof paper.

Grind the coconut with 1 tablespoon of the sugar a blender or food processor. Transfer the coconut to small bowl. Grind the almonds with 1 tablespoon of the remaining sugar in the blender or food processor; transfer the almonds to the bowl containing the coconut, and set it aside.

Sift the cornmeal, flour and baking powder into a bowl. Combine the buttermilk, lemon rind and lemon juice in a measuring jug. Cream the butter and the remaining sugar in a bowl; the mixture should be light and fluffy. Add the two eggs, one at a time, to the creamed butter and sugar, beating well after each addition. Fold in the sifted ingredients and the buttermilk alternately, adding a third of each mixture at a time. When the batter is thoroughly mixed, stir in

the ground coconut and almonds.

Spoon the batter into the prepared loaf tin. Bake the cake until a wooden toothpick inserted in the centre comes out clean — 30 to 40 minutes. Cool the tin on a rack for 10 to 15 minutes, then turn out the cake on the rack. Remove the greaseproof paper; set the cake right side up to cool.

Just before serving time, prepare the blueberry sauce. Combine the blueberries and cinnamon in a small, heavy-bottomed saucepan over medium heat. Cook the blueberries, stirring occasionally, until they pop and exude some of their juice — about 5 minutes. Serve the sauce warm — do not let it cool — with slices of cake.

Crêpes with Glazed Pears

Serves 4
Working time: about 1 hour
Total time: about 3 hours

Calories **305**
Protein **5g**
Cholesterol **80mg**
Total fat **11g**
Saturated fat **3g**
Sodium **70mg**

3	ripe pears	3
1 tbsp	fresh lemon juice	1 tbsp
½ tsp	safflower oil	½ tsp
4 tbsp	Sauternes or other sweet white wine	4 tbsp
3 tbsp	honey	3 tbsp
15 g	unsalted butter	½ oz
	freshly ground black pepper	
Sauternes crêpe batter		
7 tbsp	plain flour	7 tbsp
¹⁄₁₆ tsp	salt	¹⁄₁₆ tsp
	freshly ground black pepper	
⅛ tsp	caster sugar	⅛ tsp
1	egg	1
2 tbsp	Sauternes or other sweet white wine	2 tbsp
1½ tbsp	safflower oil	1½ tbsp
12.5 to 17.5 cl	semi-skimmed milk	4 to 6 fl oz

To prepare the crêpe batter, whisk together the flour, salt, some pepper, the sugar, egg, wine, oil and 12.5 cl (4 fl oz) of the milk in a bowl. Whisking constantly, pour in enough additional milk in a fine, steady stream to thin the batter to the consistency of double cream. Cover the bowl and refrigerate it for at least 2 hours.

Peel, core and slice the pears. Sprinkle the slices with the lemon juice and set them aside while you cook the crêpes.

Heat a crêpe pan or a 20 cm (8 inch) non-stick frying pan over medium-high heat. Pour in the ½ teaspoon of oil and spread it over the entire surface with a paper towel. Pour 2 to 3 tablespoons of the batter into the hot pan and swirl the pan just enough to coat the bottom with a thin, even layer of batter. Pour any excess batter back into the bowl. Cook the crêpe until the bottom is brown — about 30 seconds — then lift the edge of the crêpe and turn it over. Cook the second side until it is brown — about 15 seconds more — and slide the crêpe on to a plate. The crêpe should be paper thin; if it is not, stir a little more milk into the batter. Repeat the process with the remaining batter to form eight crêpes in all. If you are using a crêpe pan, you may have to oil it again to prevent sticking.

Fold a crêpe in half, then in thirds. Repeat the process to fold the remaining crêpes. Put two on each of four dessert plates, and set them aside in a warm place.

Bring the wine and honey to the boil in a sauté or frying pan over medium-high heat. Cook the mixture until it is syrupy — about 2 minutes. Add the butter and the pears, and continue cooking until the pears are barely tender and have become glazed with the mixture — about 3 minutes more.

With a slotted spoon, remove the pears from the pan and divide them evenly among the four plates. Pour a little of the syrup remaining in the pan over each portion; grind a generous amount of black pepper over all and serve at once.

Fruit-and-Nut-Filled Phyllo Roll

Serves 6
Working time: about 40 minutes
Total time: about 1 hour and 10 minutes

ories **185**		
tein **4g**		
olesterol **8mg**		
al fat **6g**		
urated fat **2g**		
dium **2mg**		

1	egg white	1
60 g	low-fat ricotta cheese	2 oz
1	orange	1
1 tsp	grated lemon rind	1 tsp
¼ tsp	ground cinnamon	¼ tsp
⅛ tsp	grated nutmeg	⅛ tsp
⅛ tsp	ground allspice	⅛ tsp
⅛ tsp	salt	⅛ tsp
3 tbsp	coarsely chopped pecan nuts	3 tbsp
75 g	raisins	2½ oz
1 tbsp	pure maple syrup	1 tbsp
4 tbsp	caster sugar	4 tbsp
2	slices wholemeal bread, toasted	2
2	sheets frozen phyllo, thawed	2
15 g	unsalted butter, melted	½ oz

To make the filling, first mix together the egg white and the ricotta. With a vegetable peeler or a paring knife, remove the rind from the orange and reserve it. Cut away all the white pith and discard it. Working over a bowl to catch the juice, segment the orange as shown on page 14, dropping the segments into the bowl. Squeeze the last drops of juice from the pulpy core of membranes into the bowl. Coarsely chop the orange rind and orange segments, and add them to the ricotta mixture along with the juice that has collected in the bowl. Stir in the lemon rind, cinnamon, nutmeg, allspice, salt, pecans, raisins, maple syrup and sugar. Cut the toasted bread slices into cubes and mix them into the filling. Set the filling aside.

Preheat the oven to 180°C (325°F or Mark 4).

Lay one of the phyllo sheets on a piece of grease-proof paper that is slightly larger than the phyllo. Lightly brush the phyllo with some of the butter. Set the second sheet of phyllo squarely on top of the first.

Spoon the filling down one of the longer sides of the double phyllo sheet, leaving about 4 cm (1½ inches) uncovered at both ends of the filling. To avoid tearing the phyllo, lift the edge of the greaseproof paper and roll the phyllo once round the filling. Continue rolling the phyllo and filling away from you to form a compact cylinder. Tuck under the two open ends of the roll and transfer it to a lightly oiled baking sheet. Brush the top of the roll with the remaining butter and bake it until it is golden-brown — about 30 minutes. Allow the roll to cool, then slice it into serving rounds.

remain white and be thoroughly dried out. Let
meringues stand at room temperature until t
cool — they will become quite crisp.

Purée the ricotta with the yogurt in a food proce
or a blender. Divide the cheese mixture among
meringue baskets, and top each with some of
strawberries and blueberries.

Rolled Cherry-Walnut Cake

Serves 8
Working time: about 1 hour
Total time: about 1 hour and 30 minutes

Calories **140**
Protein **5g**
Cholesterol **70mg**
Total fat **4g**
Saturated fat **1g**
Sodium **70mg**

30 g	shelled walnuts, finely chopped	
1½ tbsp	plain flour	1½
½ tsp	baking powder	½
2	eggs, separated, plus 1 egg white, the whites at room temperature	
2 tbsp	dark brown sugar	2
½ tsp	pure vanilla extract	½
4 tbsp	caster sugar	4
2 tsp	icing sugar	2
Cherry filling		
½ tsp	pure vanilla extract	½
¼ litre	plain low-fat yogurt	8
2 tbsp	caster sugar	2
250 g	fresh cherries, stoned (page 24) and quartered	

Berry-Filled Meringue Baskets

Serves 8
Working time: about 50 minutes
Total time: about 5 hours (includes drying)

Calories **150**
Protein **4g**
Cholesterol **5mg**
Total fat **2g**
Saturated fat **1g**
Sodium **45mg**

3	egg whites	3
200 g	caster sugar	7 oz
125 g	low-fat ricotta cheese	4 oz
4 tbsp	plain low-fat yogurt	4 tbsp
350 g	hulled, sliced strawberries	12 oz
150 g	blueberries, stemmed, picked over and rinsed	5 oz

Line a baking sheet with non-stick parchment paper or
brown paper. Preheat the oven to 70°C (160°F or Mark
¼). If your oven does not have a setting this low, set it
at its lowest. Keep the oven door propped open with a
ball of crumpled foil.

To prepare the meringue, put the egg whites and
sugar into a large, heatproof bowl. Set the bowl over a
pan of simmering water, and stir the mixture with a
whisk until the sugar has dissolved and the egg whites
are hot — about 6 minutes. Remove the bowl from
the heat. Using an electric mixer, beat the egg whites
on medium-high speed until they form stiff peaks and
have cooled to room temperature.

Transfer the meringue to a piping bag fitted with a
1 cm (½ inch) nozzle. Holding the nozzle about 1 cm
(½ inch) above the surface of the baking sheet, pipe
out the meringue in a tightly coiled spiral until you have
formed a flat disc about 8.5 cm (3½ inches) across.
Pipe a single ring of meringue on top of the edge of the
disc, forming a low wall that will hold in the filling.
Form seven more meringue baskets in the same way.

Put the baking sheet into the oven and let the meringues bake for at least 4 hours. The meringues should

Dot the corners and centre of a baking sheet w
butter. Line the sheet with greaseproof paper —
butter will hold the paper in place. Lightly butter
top of the paper, then dust it with flour and set the
aside. Heat the oven to 180°C (350°F or Mark 4).

Mix together the walnuts, flour and baking pow
in a small bowl; set the mixture aside.

Beat the two egg yolks with the brown sugar a
1½ tablespoons of very hot water until the mixtur
thick enough to fall in a ribbon when the beater is lif
from the bowl — about 4 minutes. Stir in the van
and set the bowl aside.

Beat the three egg whites on medium speed i
bowl until they form soft peaks. Increase the speec
medium high and continue beating, gradually add
the caster sugar, until stiff peaks form.

Stir about one quarter of the egg whites into
yolk mixture to lighten it. Gently fold one third of
remaining egg whites into the yolk mixture, then f
in half of the nut-and-flour mixture, followed by ha
the remaining egg whites. Finally, fold in the remain
nut-and-flour mixture and the last of the egg white

Transfer the batter to the baking sheet and sprea

out, forming a rectangle about 28 by 18 cm (11 by 7 inches). Bake the cake until it is lightly browned and springy to the touch — about 20 minutes. Let the cake cool completely — at least 30 minutes.

Sprinkle a sheet of greaseproof paper with icing sugar and invert the cake on to the paper. Gently remove the paper on which the cake baked from the bottom of the cake. Trim the edges of the cake with a serrated knife or scissors. For the filling, stir the vanilla extract into the yogurt, then spread this mixture on to the cake, leaving a 1 cm (½ inch) border uncovered all round. Sprinkle the caster sugar over the yogurt mixture, then scatter the cherries evenly on top. Starting at a long side, roll the cake into a cylinder. Set the cake on a platter; sprinkle the icing sugar over the top just before serving.

5 *Cooked briefly in the microwave, a medley of fruits in a spiced syrup heat through evenly without losing their shape or glowing colours (recipe, opposite page*

Desserts from the Microwave

Custards, puddings and fruits may seem unlikely candidates for the microwave oven, but they are only a few of the many desserts that are perfectly suited to the microwave process. When prepared conventionally, some puddings and custards require constant stirring to keep the mixture smooth and prevent it from burning. In the microwave they need be stirred only occasionally (the maple custard on page 135 is not stirred at all), and there is no danger of scorching them.

Because of their high juice content, fruits that are baked in a microwave require little added liquid — and, since they cook quickly, they lose few of their water-soluble vitamins. Fruits retain their shape, texture and much of their inviting colour as well, as in the spiced fruit salad on the right. One caution: avoid microwaving overripe fruits — they may soften to the point of disintegration.

Since some cakes fail to brown in the microwave, they are not suitable for the process. Still, cakes that have colour in themselves, such as those made with chocolate, or those with fruit at the bottom, fare very well indeed, as evidenced by the chocolate pudding cake on page 129 and the rhubarb-gingerbread upside-down cake on page 136.

The microwave oven offers another boon to cooks. It can abbreviate the time normally required for many of the simple chores associated with dessert preparation. Not only does the microwave dispense with the double boiler used for melting chocolate, but it can melt 30 g (1 oz) of chocolate in just 1½ to 2 minutes — less than one third the customary time. Similarly, hard fruit, requiring long baking in a conventional oven, softens in the microwave in minutes.

Although power settings often vary among different manufacturers' ovens, the recipes use "high" to indicate 100 per cent power, "medium high" for 70 per cent, "medium" for 50 per cent and "medium low" for 30 per cent. All custards, puddings and fruits are microwaved on high.

Hot Spiced Fruit Salad

Serves 8
Working (and total) time: about 40 minutes

Calories **160**
Protein **1g**
Cholesterol **0mg**
Total fat **0g**
Saturated fat **0g**
Sodium **10mg**

1	orange, rind thinly pared, in one long spiral if possible	1
¼ litre	fresh orange juice	8 fl oz
½ tsp	ground ginger	½ tsp
8	cardamom pods, crushed	8
5 cm	piece of cinnamon stick	2 inch
125 g	soft light brown sugar	4 oz
1	mango, peeled, stoned, flesh cut into thin slices (box, page 29)	1
1	papaya, cut in half, seeds and skin removed, flesh cut lengthwise into thin slices	1
½	pineapple, skin removed (page 28, Steps 1 and 2), flesh cut lengthwise into thin slices, core discarded	½
2	large peaches, blanched for 30 seconds, peeled, stoned and cut into 8 sections	2
2	plums, stoned and quartered	2
2	kiwi fruits, peeled and sliced	2

Put the orange rind, orange juice, ginger, cardamom, cinnamon and brown sugar into a large bowl. Stir thoroughly, then microwave the mixture on high for 4 minutes, stirring after 2 minutes.

Add the mango, papaya and pineapple slices to the orange juice mixture and microwave on high for 2 minutes. Add the peaches, plums and kiwi fruits and microwave for a further 3 to 4 minutes, stirring twice, until the fruits are heated through but not overcooked. Serve the fruit salad hot.

Gooseberries with a Dumpling Topping

Serves 4
Working time: about 30 minutes
Total time: about 40 minutes

Calories **230**
Protein **2g**
Cholesterol **10mg**
Total fat **3g**
Saturated fat **2g**
Sodium **310mg**

500 g	fresh gooseberries, picked over, or frozen gooseberries, thawed	1 lb
100 g	sugar	3½ oz
¼ tsp	ground cinnamon	¼ tsp
⅛ tsp	grated nutmeg	⅛ tsp
½ tbsp	fresh lemon juice	½ tbsp
Dumpling topping		
100 g	plain flour	3½ oz
1 tbsp	sugar	1 tbsp
½ tbsp	baking powder	½ tbsp
⅛ tsp	salt	⅛ tsp
½	lemon, grated rind only	½
1 tbsp	cold unsalted butter	1 tbsp
12.5 cl	semi-skimmed milk	4 fl oz

Mix the gooseberries, sugar, cinnamon, nutmeg and lemon juice in a 1.5 litre (2½ pint) soufflé dish or baking dish. Cover the dish and microwave it on high for 2 minutes. Set the dish aside, still covered.

For the topping, combine the flour, sugar, baking powder, salt and lemon rind in a food processor. Cut the butter into the dry ingredients, then blend in the milk. (Alternatively, prepare the topping in a bowl, cutting the butter into the dry ingredients with a pastry cutter and blending in the milk with a wooden spoon.) Stop mixing the topping as soon as the milk is incorporated.

Drop the topping on to the gooseberries in four rounded tablespoonfuls. Microwave the gooseberries, uncovered, on medium (50 per cent power) for 6 minutes, turning the dish after 3 minutes. Let the dessert stand for 2 minutes before serving.

Chocolate Pudding Cake

Serves 10
Working time: about 20 minutes
Total time: about 40 minutes

Calories **190**
Protein **3g**
Cholesterol **1mg**
Total fat **5g**
Saturated fat **1g**
Sodium **150mg**

165 g	caster sugar	5½ oz
125 g	plain flour	4 oz
¼ tsp	salt	¼ tsp
6 tbsp	unsweetened cocoa powder	6 tbsp
2 tsp	baking powder	2 tsp
12.5 cl	semi-skimmed milk	4 fl oz
2 tbsp	safflower oil	2 tbsp
1½ tsp	pure vanilla extract	1½ tsp
30 g	shelled walnuts, chopped	1 oz
6 tbsp	light brown sugar	6 tbsp
1 tbsp	icing sugar	1 tbsp

Lightly butter a 23 cm (9 inch) pie dish and dust it with cocoa powder.

In a bowl, sift together 100 g (3½ oz) of the caster sugar, the flour, salt, 3 tablespoons of the cocoa powder and the baking powder. Add the milk, oil and 1 teaspoon of the vanilla extract, then stir to combine the liquid ingredients with the dry. Stir in the walnuts, and spread the cake batter evenly in the pie dish.

Mix together the remaining caster sugar, the remaining 3 tablespoons of cocoa powder and the brown sugar. Stir in the remaining ½ teaspoon of vanilla extract and ¼ litre (8 fl oz) of water. Pour this liquid over the batter in the pie dish.

Microwave the cake on medium (50 per cent power) for 18 to 20 minutes, rotating the dish a quarter turn every 3 minutes. Serve the cake warm. Just before serving, sift the icing sugar on to the cake.

Vanilla Custard with Yogurt and Apricots

Serves 10
Working time: about 30 minutes
Total time: about 1 hour and 30 minutes
(includes chilling)

Calories **205**
Protein **6g**
Cholesterol **65mg**
Total fat **3g**
Saturated fat **2g**
Sodium **110mg**

125 g	dried apricots, coarsely chopped	4 oz
200 g	plus 1 tbsp sugar	7 oz
6 tbsp	cornflour	6 tbsp
⅛ tsp	salt	⅛ tsp
1 litre	semi-skimmed milk	1¾ pints
5 cm	length of vanilla pod, split lengthwise, or 1 tsp pure vanilla extract	2 inch
2	eggs, beaten	2
17.5 cl	plain low-fat yogurt	6 fl oz

Combine the apricots with 12.5 cl (4 fl oz) of water and 1 tablespoon of the sugar in a glass bowl. Cover the bowl and microwave the mixture on high, stopping midway to stir it, until the apricots are tender — 4 to 6 minutes. Purée the mixture in a food processor or a blender, then return the purée to the bowl. Cover the bowl and refrigerate it.

Combine the cornflour, salt and the remaining sugar in a small bowl. Pour the milk into a 2 litre (3½ pint) glass bowl and add the cornflour mixture. Whisk the mixture until the cornflour is completely dissolved. Add the vanilla pod, if you are using it. Microwave the mixture on high, stopping once or twice to stir it, until the milk is hot — about 8 minutes.

If you are using the vanilla pod, remove it from the milk and scrape the seeds inside it into the milk. Discard the pod.

Whisk about 12.5 cl (4 fl oz) of the hot milk into the eggs. Immediately whisk the egg-milk mixture — and the vanilla extract, if you are using it — into the remaining hot milk. Microwave the mixture on high for 3 minutes. Whisk the mixture and continue cooking it on high, whisking every 60 seconds, until it thickens — 2 to 3 minutes more. Divide the custard among 10 dessert cups and put them into the refrigerator for at least 1 hour.

Just before serving, spread a dollop of yogurt over each custard and top it with the apricot purée.

EDITOR'S NOTE: *This custard may be prepared up to 24 hours before it is served.*

Baked Apples Filled with Cranberries and Sultanas

Serves 6
Working time: about 20 minutes
Total time: about 40 minutes

Calories **210**
Protein **1g**
Cholesterol **8mg**
Total fat **4g**
Saturated fat **2g**
Sodium **8mg**

250 g	fresh or frozen cranberries	8 oz
90 g	light brown sugar	3 oz
3 tbsp	sultanas, chopped	3 tbsp
25 g	unsalted butter	¾ oz
6	Golden Delicious apples	6

Put the cranberries into a glass bowl and sprinkle the brown sugar over them. Cover the bowl with plastic film and microwave the berries on high for 2 minutes. Stir in the sultanas and 15 g (½ oz) of the butter, recover the bowl, and cook the mixture on high until the berries start to burst — 1½ to 2½ minutes. Stir the mixture well and set it aside.

Core one of the apples with a melon baller or a small spoon, scooping out the centre of the apple to form a conical cavity about 3 cm (1¼ inches) wide at the top and only 1 cm (½ inch) wide at the bottom. Using a cannelle knife or a paring knife, cut two grooves for decoration round the apple. Prepare the other apples the same way.

Fill the apples with the cranberry mixture. Arrange the apples in a ring round the edge of a glass pie plate

and dot them with the remaining butter. Cover the filled apples with greaseproof paper and microwave them on high for 5 minutes. Rotate the plate and each apple 180 degrees, and microwave the apples on high for 3 to 5 minutes more. Let the apples stand for about 5 minutes before serving them with their baking juices ladled over the top.

Coffee Soufflé

Serves 8
Working time: about 15 minutes
Total time: about 25 minutes

Calories **100**
Protein **4g**
Cholesterol **5mg**
Total fat **2g**
Saturated fat **1g**
Sodium **60mg**

100 g	caster sugar	3½ oz
15 g	unsalted butter	½ oz
3 tbsp	plain flour	3 tbsp
2 tsp	instant coffee, mixed with 2 tbsp boiling water	2 tsp
2 tbsp	cointreau or other orange-flavoured liqueur (optional)	2 tbsp
1 tsp	pure vanilla extract	1 tsp
17.5 cl	evaporated milk	6 fl oz
5	egg whites, at room temperature	5
	chocolate coffee-bean sweets (optional)	

Lightly butter the inside of a 1.25 litre (2 pint) soufflé dish. Put about 2 teaspoons of the sugar into the dish, then rotate the dish, tilting it in all directions to coat its sides and bottom. Refrigerate the dish.

Put the butter into a 2 litre (3½ pint) glass bowl. Microwave it on high until the butter melts — about 45 seconds. Whisk the flour into the butter to form a smooth paste. Add the coffee, the liqueur if you are using it, and the vanilla extract. Whisk the coffee base until it is smooth again, then stir in the evaporated milk, and microwave it on high for 1½ minutes. Stir the coffee base; microwave it on high until it has thickened — about 1 minute more. Whisk the coffee base once more, then add all but 2 tablespoons of the remaining sugar. Mix thoroughly and set the bowl aside.

In a separate bowl, beat the egg whites until they form soft peaks. Add the remaining 2 tablespoons of sugar a little at a time, beating continuously until the whites are shiny and hold stiff peaks.

Stir one quarter of the whites into the coffee base to lighten it. Gently — but quickly — fold the coffee base into the remaining whites. Spoon the mixture into the buttered dish, then microwave it on medium low (30 per cent power) for 10 to 12 minutes, rotating the dish a quarter turn every 3 minutes. The soufflé should rise about 2.5 cm (1 inch) above the rim of the dish and appear set. Serve the soufflé immediately, garnished, if you like, with the coffee-bean sweets.

Mocha Pudding

Serves 6
Working time: about 20 minutes
Total time: about 1 hour and 20 minutes
(includes chilling)

Calories **220**
Protein **5g**
Cholesterol **11mg**
Total fat **7g**
Saturated fat **4g**
Sodium **110mg**

45 g	plain chocolate	1½ oz
60 cl	semi-skimmed milk	1 pint
12.5 cl	double-strength coffee	4 fl oz
4 tbsp	cornflour	4 tbsp
150 g	caster sugar	5 oz
⅛ tsp	salt	⅛ tsp
3 tbsp	half cream, half milk	3 tbsp

Place the chocolate in a 2 litre (3½ pint) glass bowl and cook it on medium (50 per cent power) for 2 to 3 minutes. (Though the chocolate will appear not to have melted, it will be soft.) Whisk the milk and coffee into the chocolate. Combine the cornflour, sugar and salt, and whisk them into the milk mixture. Microwave the contents of the bowl on high for 4 minutes. Whisk the mixture and continue cooking it on high, whisking every 60 seconds, until it thickens — 4 to 6 minutes more. Pour the pudding into six dessert cups and refrigerate them for at least 1 hour.

Just before serving the pudding, dribble ½ tablespoon of the cream-milk mixture over each portion.

Tapioca-Rum Pudding with Orange

Serves 6
Working time: about 30 minutes
Total time: about 1 hour and 30 minutes
(includes chilling)

Calories **155**
Protein **5g**
Cholesterol **50mg**
Total fat **3g**
Saturated fat **1g**
Sodium **105mg**

1	egg, separated, the white at room temperature	1
½ litre	semi-skimmed milk	16 fl oz
2 tbsp	white rum	2 tbsp
4 tbsp	instant tapioca	4 tbsp
5 tbsp	caster sugar	5 tbsp
1 tsp	grated orange rind	1 tsp
⅛ tsp	salt	⅛ tsp
2	oranges	2

Whisk together the egg yolk, milk and rum in a 2 litre (3½ pint) glass bowl. Stir in the tapioca, 3 tablespoons of the sugar, the orange rind and the salt, and allow the mixture to stand for 5 minutes to soften the tapioca.

Microwave the mixture on high, stopping three or four times to whisk it, until it thickens — 6 to 8 minutes. Remove the bowl from the oven and set it aside while you prepare the meringue.

In a bowl, beat the egg white until soft peaks form. Beating continuously, gradually add the remaining 2 tablespoons of sugar; continue beating the meringue until it forms stiff peaks.

Mix about one third of the meringue into the tapioca mixture to lighten it, then gently fold in the remaining meringue. Spoon the pudding into six dessert cups and refrigerate them until the dessert has cooled — approximately 1 hour.

While the pudding cools, peel and segment the oranges *(page 14)*. Garnish each pudding with a few orange segments just before serving.

Maple Custard
with Walnuts

Serves 4
Working time: about 15 minutes
Total time: about 1 hour (includes cooling)

Calories **155**
Protein **7g**
Cholesterol **75mg**
Total fat **4g**
Saturated fat **2g**
Sodium **100mg**

1	egg, plus 2 egg whites	1
100 g	maple syrup	3½ oz
1 tsp	pure vanilla extract	1 tsp
35 cl	semi-skimmed milk	12 fl oz
4	walnut halves	4

In a large bowl, whisk together the egg, egg whites, maple syrup and vanilla extract. Pour in the milk and continue whisking the mixture until the eggs are completely blended in.

Pour the mixture into four 12.5 cl (4 fl oz) baking dishes or ramekins. Microwave the custards on medium (50 per cent power), rearranging the dishes every 3 minutes, just until the custards set — about 7 minutes in all. Allow the custards to cool to room temperature before transferring them to the refrigerator.

Serve the custards still in their dishes or unmould them first. Present each one with a walnut half on top.

Place a flat, straight-edged object — a spatula, for example, or a piece of cardboard — over one half of a toast triangle and use a sieve to dust the exposed portion with some of the icing sugar. Repeat the process to dust the remaining toast triangles, and serve them with the rhubarb-apple sauce.

Rhubarb-Apple Sauce with Sugar Toast

Serves 6
Working time: about 25 minutes
Total time: about 40 minutes

Calories **205**
Protein **2g**
Cholesterol **5mg**
Total fat **3g**
Saturated fat **1g**
Sodium **60mg**

750 g	tart green apples, peeled, cored and coarsely chopped	1½ lb
1 tbsp	fresh lemon juice	1 tbsp
250 g	fresh rhubarb, finely chopped, or frozen rhubarb, thawed and finely chopped	8 oz
100 g	caster sugar	3½ oz
4 tbsp	dry sherry	4 tbsp
⅛ tsp	grated nutmeg	⅛ tsp
3	slices white bread, crusts removed	3
15 g	unsalted butter	½ oz
2 tbsp	icing sugar	2 tbsp

Toss the chopped apple with the lemon juice in a 2 litre (3½ pint) baking dish. Add the rhubarb, sugar, sherry and nutmeg. Cover the dish and microwave it on high for 10 to 12 minutes, stirring the mixture every 3 minutes. The rhubarb and apples should be very tender.

Meanwhile, to make the sugar toast, cut each slice of bread diagonally into two triangles. Melt the butter in a heavy frying pan over medium heat. Lightly brush both sides of each bread triangle with the butter. Place the triangles in the pan and cook them until they have browned. Transfer the toast to a rack to cool.

Rhubarb-Gingerbread Upside-Down Cake

Serves 8
Working time: about 20 minutes
Total time: about 50 minutes

Calories **200**
Protein **4g**
Cholesterol **40mg**
Total fat **4g**
Saturated fat **2g**
Sodium **200mg**

30 g	unsalted butter	1 o
6 tbsp	light brown sugar	6 tbs
250 g	fresh rhubarb, coarsely chopped, or frozen rhubarb, thawed, coarsely chopped	8 o
140 g	plain flour	5 o
60 g	wholemeal flour	2 o
1 tsp	bicarbonate of soda	1 ts
1 tsp	ground ginger	1 ts
1 tsp	ground cinnamon	1 ts
½ tsp	grated nutmeg	½ ts
¼ tsp	dry mustard	¼ ts
¼ tsp	ground cloves	¼ ts
¼ tsp	salt	¼ ts
1	egg	
165 g	dark molasses	5½ o
1 tsp	pure vanilla extract	1 ts

Put the butter into a 23 cm (9 inch) glass pie plate an microwave it on high for 45 seconds. Smear it ove the bottom of the plate, coating it evenly, then sprink in the brown sugar. Scatter the rhubarb over the suga

In a large bowl, combine the plain flour, wholeme flour, bicarbonate of soda, ginger, cinnamon, nutme mustard, cloves and salt. In a second bowl, mix the egg, molasses, vanilla and 12.5 cl (4 fl oz) of hot water.

Stir the liquid into the dry ingredients, forming a smooth batter. Pour the batter into the pie plate and microwave it on high for 10 minutes, turning the dish every 3 minutes.

Remove the cake from the oven and let it stand for 5 minutes. Run the tip of a knife round the sides of the cake. Invert a serving plate on top of the pie plate and turn both over together; do not remove the pie plate. Let the cake stand for 5 minutes more, then lift away the pie plate. The cake is best served warm.

EDITOR'S NOTE: *This cake is also an ideal showcase for other fruits. Coarsely chopped plums, sour cherries or peeled pears might be substituted for the rhubarb.*

Glossary

Allspice: the dried berry of a member of the myrtle family. Used whole or ground, it is called allspice because its flavour resembles a combination of clove, cinnamon and nutmeg.

Almond paste: a mixture of ground almonds and sugar, used in making pastry fillings and toppings as well as biscuits and sweets.

Amaretto: an almond-flavoured liqueur.

Armagnac: a dry brandy, often more strongly flavoured than cognac, from the Armagnac district of south-west France.

Arrowroot: a tasteless, starchy, white powder refined from the root of a tropical plant; it is used to thicken puddings and sauces. Unlike flour, it is transparent when cooked.

Baking powder: a raising agent that releases carbon dioxide during baking, causing cake or biscuit batter to rise. Ordinary baking powders, as used in these recipes, have a high sodium content, but sodium-free baking powder is available for people on low-sodium diets.

Balsamic vinegar: a mildly acid, intensely fragrant wine-based vinegar made in northern Italy. Traditionally it is aged in wooden casks.

Bavarian: classically, a cold, rich dessert made with custard and whipped cream, and set with gelatine. The lighter version in this book uses Italian meringue and yogurt.

Bombe: a dessert with several layers of different flavours and colours of ice cream or sorbet, frozen in a small round mould.

Brûlée: a French adjective based on the verb "bruler" (to burn); used to describe the caramelized topping on a dessert.

Buttermilk: a tangy, cultured-milk product that, despite its name, contains about one third less fat than whole milk.

Calorie (or kilocalorie): a precise measure of the energy food supplies when it is broken down for use in the body.

Cappuccino: espresso mixed with hot frothed milk or cream, and a flavouring, usually cinnamon.

Carambola: an edible fruit from south-east Asia, with translucent orange or yellow flesh. It has a five-sided, ribbed structure and makes an attractive garnish when cut crosswise into star-shaped slices.

Caramelize: to heat sugar, or a food naturally rich in sugar such as fruit, until the sugar turns brown and syrupy.

Cardamom: the bittersweet, aromatic dried seeds or whole pods of a plant in the ginger family.

Cholesterol: a waxlike substance that is manufactured in the human body and also found in foods of animal origin. Although a certain amount of cholesterol is necessary for proper body functioning, an excess can accumulate in the arteries, contributing to heart disease. See also Monounsaturated fats; Polyunsaturated fats; Saturated fats.

Choux paste: a pastry dough, made from water or milk, butter, flour and eggs, that puffs up in the oven when it is baked. The recipes for choux paste in this book replace some of the egg yolk traditionally called for with egg white and use safflower oil instead of butter to reduce cholesterol.

Churn-freezing: preparing a frozen dessert by stirring it continuously with a paddle during the freezing process.

Cobbler: a moist, deep-dish fruit dessert that resembles a pie but lacks a bottom crust. In traditional cobblers, the crust consists of scone dough.

Cocoa powder: the result of pulverizing roasted cocoa beans, then removing most of the fat, or cocoa butter.

Coeur à fromage mould: a heart-shaped mould, with holes to drain excess liquid, used when making *coeur à fromage* or *coeur à la crème*.

Cornflour: a starchy white powder made from corn kernels and used to thicken many puddings and sauces. Like arrowroot, it is transparent when cooked and makes a more efficient thickener than flour. When cooked conventionally, a liquid containing cornflour must be stirred constantly in the early stages to prevent lumps from forming.

Cream of tartar: a natural, mild acid in powder form with a slightly sour taste, used to stabilize beaten egg whites. It should be used sparingly — no more than ⅛ teaspoon to one egg white. Beating egg whites in a copper bowl has a similar stabilizing effect.

Crème de cassis: an alcoholic cordial made from blackcurrants.

Crêpe: a paper-thin pancake that can accommodate a variety of fillings, among them fruit purées and poached fruit. Often served with a sauce or a wine or spirit-based syrup.

Crumble: a dessert of cooked fruit with a crumbly topping that is baked to make it crisp.

Crystallized ginger: the spicy, rootlike stems of ginger preserved with sugar. Crystallized ginger should not be confused with ginger in syrup.

Espresso: very strong coffee made by forcing a combination of steam and water through an especially dark and powdery grind of coffee beans.

Fat: a basic component of many foods, comprising three types of fatty acid — saturated, monounsaturated and polyunsaturated — in varying proportions. See also Monounsaturated fats; Polyunsaturated fats; Saturated fats.

Filbert: see Hazelnut.

Gelatine: a virtually tasteless protein, available in powdered form or in sheets. Dissolved gelatine is used to set chilled desserts so that they retain their shape when unmoulded.

Gewürztraminer (also called Traminer): a flowery white wine with a particular affinity for fruit.

Ginger: the spicy, buff-coloured, rootlike stem of the ginger plant, used as a seasoning either fresh or dried and powdered. The dried form should never be substituted for the fresh. See also Crystallized ginger.

Glaze: to coat the surface of a tart or cake with a thin, shiny layer of melted jam or caramel.

Grand Marnier: a high-quality liqueur made from cognac and orange peel, which has a distinctive orange flavour.

Green peppercorns: the small, round, unripened berries of the pepper vine, preserved in water or vinegar. Their taste is less pronounced than that of dried black or white peppercorns.

Grenadine: a sweet, deep red syrup made from pomegranates and sugar; used as a colouring as well as a flavouring in cold desserts and in drinks.

Hazelnut: the fruit of a shrublike tree found primarily in Turkey, Italy and Spain, and in the United States. Filberts, which are cultivated, have a stronger flavour than hazelnuts, which grow wild. Both are prized by bakers and sweetmakers.

Icing sugar: finely ground granulated sugar, with a small amount of added cornflour to ensure a powdery consistency. The sugar's ability to dissolve instantly makes it ideal for desserts in which a grainy texture is undesirable.

Italian meringue: a type of meringue created by beating together hot sugar syrup and egg whites. Italian meringue is used in this book as the basis for mousses, parfaits and cheesecakes, and as a substitute for whipped cream. See also Meringue.

Julienne: the French term for food cut into thin strips.

Kirsch (also called Kirschwasser): a clear cherry brandy distilled from small black cherries grown in Switzerland, Germany and the Alsace region of France; often used to macerate fruit desserts.

Kiwi fruit: an egg-shaped fruit with a fuzzy brown skin, tart, lime green flesh and hundreds of tiny black edible seeds. Peeled and sliced, the kiwi displays a starburst of seeds at its centre that lends a decorative note to tarts and other desserts.

Kugel: a noodle pudding cooked in a casserole or a frying pan.

Kugelhopf mould: a decoratively fluted tube-cake tin. The tube conducts heat into the centre of the batter, ensuring even cooking.

Mace: the ground aril, or covering, that encases the nutmeg seed, widely used as a flavouring agent in baking.

Macerate: to soak a food – usually fruit – in sweetened lemon juice, wine or liqueur until the food softens and absorbs the flavours of the liquid.

Madeleine tray: a specialized mould with scallop-shaped indentations, designed for making small cakes but used in this book for moulding sorbet.

Mango: a fruit grown throughout the tropics, with sweet, succulent, yellow-orange flesh that is extremely rich in vitamin A. Like papaya, it may cause an allergic reaction in some individuals.

Melon baller: a kitchen tool with a sharp-edged, stainless-steel scoop at each end; it is used to cut perfect spheres of flesh from melons and other fruit.

Meringue: an airy concoction made from stiffly beaten egg whites and sugar. It serves as the base for mousses and soufflés and is folded into angel food and chiffon cake batters. Meringue may also be baked to produce edible baskets for ice cream or other frozen fillings. See also Italian meringue.

Mocha: a flavouring made by combining chocolate and coffee.

Monounsaturated fats: one of the three types of fat found in foods. Monounsaturated fats are believed not to raise the level of cholesterol in the blood.

Mousse: a chilled, sometimes frozen, dish with a light, creamy texture. Traditionally it is composed of a flavoured base aerated with beaten egg whites, whipped cream or both.

Navel orange: a seedless orange characterized by the navel-like indentation opposite its stem end. It is particularly easy to peel and segment.

Non-reactive pan or bowl: a cooking vessel whose

face does not react chemically with food. Materials ...ed include ovenproof clay, stainless steel, enamel, ...ss and aluminium that has been finished with a ...n-stick coating. Untreated cast iron and aluminium ...y react with acids , producing discoloration or a ...culiar taste.

...**paya** (also called pawpaw): a pear-shaped, ...elon-like tropical fruit rich in vitamins A and C. Like ...ngo, it may cause an allergic reaction in some ...dividuals.

...**rchment paper:** a re-usable paper treated with ...cone to produce a non-stick surface. It is used to ...e cake tins and baking sheets, and to wrap foods ...baking.

...**ssion fruit:** a juicy, fragrant, egg-shaped tropical ...it with wrinkled skin, yellow flesh and many small ...ck seeds. The seeds are edible; the skin is not.

...**yllo** (also spelt "filo"): a paper-thin ...ur-and-water pastry popular in Greece and the ...ddle East. It can be made at home or bought, fresh ...frozen, from delicatessens and shops specializing ...Middle-Eastern food. Because frozen phyllo dries ...t easily, it should be thawed in the refrigerator, and ...y phyllo sheets not in use should be covered with ...amp towel.

...**ntain:** a starchy variety of banana that is normally ...ked before it is eaten. Although the skin turns ...lowish-brown and then black as the plantain ripens, ...e flesh remains creamy yellow or slightly pink.

...**ach:** to cook a food in barely simmering liquid as a ...ans of preserving moisture and adding flavour. ...it may be poached in wine or a light syrup.

...**lyunsaturated fats:** one of the three types of fats ...und in foods. They exist in abundance in such ...getable oils as safflower, sunflower, corn and soya ...an. Polyunsaturated fats lower the level of ...olesterol in the blood.

...**ppy seeds:** the spherical black seeds produced by ...ariety of poppy plant, and used as an ingredient or ...pping in cakes. Poppy seeds are so small that ...0 g (1 lb) of them numbers nearly a million seeds.

...**rée:** to reduce food to a smooth, even, pulplike ...nsistency by mashing it, passing it through a sieve, ...processing it in a food processor or a blender.

...**ark:** a type of soft cheese with a mild, clean, ...ghtly acid flavour; usually low in fat, but smoother ...rieties have added cream.

...**mekin:** a small, round, straight-sided glass or porcelain mould used to hold a single portion of food.

Recommended Daily Amount (RDA): the average daily amount of an essential nutrient recommended for healthy people by the U.K. Department of Health and Social Security.

Reduce: to boil down a liquid in order to concentrate its flavour or thicken its consistency.

Ricotta: soft, mild, white Italian cheese, made from cow's or sheep's milk. Full-fat ricotta has a fat content of 20 to 30 per cent, but the low-fat ricotta in the recipes in this book has a fat content of only about 8 per cent.

Rind: the flavourful outermost layer of citrus-fruit peel; it should be cut or grated free of the white pith that lies beneath it.

Rolled oats: a cereal made from oats that have been ground into meal, then steamed, rolled into flakes and dried.

Ruby port: a ruby-coloured sweet dessert wine, originally from the Portuguese seaside town of Oporto, fortified with a small amount of brandy and usually aged in wooden casks.

Sabayon: a foamy sauce made by beating eggs with a liquid, such as wine, over heat. A sweetened sabayon often serves as a topping for fruit gratins.

Safflower oil: a vegetable oil that contains the highest proportion of polyunsaturated fats.

Saturated fats: one of the three types of fats found in foods. They exist in abundance in animal products and coconut and palm oils; they raise the level of cholesterol in the blood. Because high blood-cholesterol levels may cause heart disease, saturated fat consumption should be restricted to less than 15 per cent of the calories provided by the daily diet.

Sauternes: a sweet, full-bodied table wine made in the Sauternes district of France. The best Sauternes are among the longest-lived and most expensive of French wines; less expensive Sauternes, however, are quite suitable for use in cooking.

Sodium: a nutrient essential to maintaining the proper balance of fluids in the body. In most diets, a major source of the element is table salt, which contains 40 per cent sodium. Excess sodium may contribute to high blood pressure, which increases the risk of heart disease. One teaspoon (5.5 g) of salt, with 2,132 milligrams of sodium, contains just over the maximum daily amount recommended by the World Health Organization.

Sorbet: a frozen mixture of fruit purée or juice, sugar and often water that may be served as a dessert or as a refreshing interlude between courses. It may also contain egg white.

Springform tin: a round tin with removable sides, designed to hold desserts, such as cheesecake, that cannot be unmoulded.

Streusel: a filling or topping for desserts, usually made by combining flour, butter, sugar and flavourings to form coarse crumbs.

Tapioca: an easily digestible starch derived from the fleshy root of a tropical plant. Tapioca thickens when it is heated in liquid.

Terrine: a loaf-shaped earthenware casserole, or the delicacy that is cooked in one.

Timbale: a small, usually drum-shaped, baking dish or its contents.

Torte: classically, a rich cake with crumbs or ground nuts replacing all or part of the flour. The frozen version in this book calls for sorbet and meringue.

Total fat: an individual's daily intake of polyunsaturated, monounsaturated and saturated fats. Nutritionists recommend that total fat constitute no more than 35 per cent of the energy in the diet. The term as used in this book refers to the combined fats in a given dish or food.

Vanilla extract: pure vanilla extract is the flavouring obtained by macerating vanilla pods in an alcohol solution. Artificial vanilla flavouring is chemically synthesized from clove oil.

Vanilla pod: the fermented and cured pod of a climbing orchid, native to Central America, used to flavour desserts. The whole pod may be steeped in a liquid, or the pod may be split and the tiny black seeds inside scraped out for use as the flavouring.

White peppercorns: the dried cores of fully ripened berries harvested from the tropical pepper vine. White peppercorns are milder than black peppercorns; many cooks prefer them for light-coloured foods and sauces.

Yogurt: a smooth-textured, semi-solid cultured milk product made with varying percentages of fat. Yogurt may be frozen with fruit and eaten as a dessert. It can also be substituted for soured cream in cooking or be combined with soured cream to produce a sauce or topping that is lower in fat and calories than soured cream alone. An alternative is to use thick Greek-style strained yogurt. This contains 10 per cent fat, as compared to 18 per cent in soured cream.

Index

Picture Credits

photographs in this book were taken by staff
otographer Renée Comet unless otherwise
dicated:

ver: James Murphy. 2: top, Scarlet Cheng; centre,
rolyn Wall Rothery. 4: lower left, Rina Ganassa. 5:
per right, Michael Latil. 6: courtesy Harris Country
ritage Society, Houston, Tex. 14: top, Lisa Masson;

bottom, Michael Latil. 15-17: Lisa Masson. 19: Lisa
Masson. 21: Lisa Masson. 23: Lisa Masson. 24: right,
Taran Z. 26: Rina Ganassa. 28: Taran Z. 29: bottom,
Michael Latil. 30: Michael Latil. 32: Lisa Masson. 34:
Lisa Masson. 35: Taran Z. 37, 38: Lisa Masson. 44:
Michael Latil. 45: top, Taran Z; bottom, Michael Latil.
46, 47: Michael Latil. 50: Martin Brigdale. 56:
bottom, Michael Latil. 80: Michael Latil. 82-83:

techniques, Taran Z; biscuits, Michael Latil. 94:
Rina Ganassa. 95: top, Michael Latil. 99: Michael
Latil. 103: top, Michael Latil. 106, 107: Martin
Brigdale. 108, 109: Michael Latil. 110: John Elliott.
111-113: Michael Latil. 115, 116: Michael Latil. 118,
119: John Elliott. 124: Michael Latil. 126: Martin
Brigdale. 128: John Elliott. 131: Michael Latil. 135:
Steven Biver.

Acknowledgements

e editors are particularly indebted to the following
ople for creating recipes for this volume: Mary Jane
ndford, Sarah Brash and Peter Brett, Alexandria,
; U.S.A.; Nora Carey, Paris; Robert Chambers,
w York, N.Y.; Carole Clements, London; Shirley
rriher, Alexandria, Va., U.S.A.; Sharon Farrington,
hesda, Md., U.S.A.; Carol Gvozdich, Alexandria,
, U.S.A.; Andrea Lambton, London; Nancy
dved, Alexandria, Va., U.S.A.; Rebecca Marshall,
w York, N.Y.; Wendye Pardue, New Canaan,
nn., U.S.A.; Paula S. Rothberg, Jane Sigal and
nette Smyth, Alexandria, Va., U.S.A.; Richard
nell, Hoboken, N.J., U.S.A.; Peter Staehli,
thersburg, Md., U.S.A.; Kathleen Stang,
shington, D.C.; Rita Walters, London; Sarah
ey, London; CiCi Williamson and Ann Steiner,
xandria, Va., U.S.A.; Jolene Worthington,
cago, Ill., U.S.A.

editors also wish to thank: Jo Calabrese, Royal
rcester Spode Inc., New York, N.Y.; Jackie

Chalkley, Fine Crafts and Wearables, Washington,
D.C.; Nic Colling, Home Produce Company,
Alexandria, Va., U.S.A.; Margaret Berry Cotton,
Hanover, N.H., U.S.A.; Cuisinarts, Inc., Greenwich,
Conn., U.S.A.; La Cuisine, Alexandria, Va., U.S.A.;
Jeanne Dale, The Pilgrim Glass Corp., New York, N.Y.;
Rex Downey, Oxon Hill, Md., U.S.A.; Flowers Unique,
Alexandria, Va., U.S.A.; Flying Foods, International,
Long Island City, N.Y., U.S.A.; Dennis Garrett, Ed
Nash, The American Hand Plus, Washington, D.C.;
Giant Foods, Inc., Landover, Md., U.S.A.; Judith
Goodkind, Alexandria, Va., U.S.A.; Chong Su Han,
Grass Roots Restaurant, Alexandria, Va., U.S.A.; Joe
Huffer, Mount Solon, Va., U.S.A.; Imperial Produce,
Washington, D.C.; Kitchen Bazaar, Washington,
D.C.; KitchenAid, Inc., Troy, Ohio, U.S.A.; Kossow
Gourmet Produce, Washington, D.C.; Gary Latzman,
Kirk Phillips, Retroneu, New York, N.Y.; Magruder's,
Inc., Rockville, Md., U.S.A.; Sara Mark, Alexandria,
Va., U.S.A.; Nambé Mills Inc., Santa Fe, N.Mex.,
U.S.A.; Andrew Naylor, Alexandria, Va., U.S.A.; Hiu

Newcomb, Potomac Vegetable Farms, Vienna, Va.,
U.S.A.; Northwest Cherry Growers; Oster,
Milwaukee, Wis., U.S.A.; Lisa Ownby, Alexandria,
Va., U.S.A.; Joyce Piotrowski, Vienna, Va., U.S.A.; C.
Kyle and Ruth Randall, Alexandria, Va., U.S.A.; Linda
Robertson, JUD Tile, Vienna, Va., U.S.A.; Safeway
Stores, Inc., Landover, Md., U.S.A.; Bert Saunders,
WILTON Armetale, New York, N.Y., U.S.A.; Schiller and
Asmus, Inc., Yemasse, S.C., U.S.A.; Sid and Betty
Solomon, Capitol Restaurant Equipment Co.,
Washington, D.C.; Nancy Snyder, Snyder's Sprouts,
Rockville, Md., U.S.A.; Straight from the Crate, Inc.,
Alexandria, Va., U.S.A.; Sutton Place Gourmet,
Washington, D.C.; Kathy Swekel, Columbia, Md.,
U.S.A.; Nancy Teksten, National Onion Association,
Greeley, Colo., U.S.A.; United Fresh Fruit and
Vegetable Association, Alexandria, Va., U.S.A.; U.S.
Fish, Kensington, Md., U.S.A.; Albert Uster Imports,
Gaithersburg, Md., U.S.A.; Williams-Sonoma, Inc.,
Alexandria, Va., U.S.A.; Lynn Addison Yorke,
Cheverly, Md., U.S.A.

our separations by Fotolitomec, S.N.C., Milan, Italy
esetting by G. Beard and Son Ltd, Brighton, Sussex, England
ted and bound by Oriental Press, Dubai